Black Undergraduates from *Bakke* to *Grutter*:

FRESHMEN STATUS, TRENDS AND PROSPECTS, 1971–2004

Walter R. Allen
Uma M. Jayakumar
Kimberly A. Griffin
William S. Korn
Sylvia Hurtado

Acknowledgments: Preparation of this report was partially funded by a grant from the Lumina Foundation and the Andrew W. Mellon Foundation. The Allan Murray Cartter endowment at the UCLA Graduate School of Education & Information Studies and the Ralph J. Bunche Center for African American Studies at UCLA also provided support. Ophella Dano provided typing and editorial assistance. The National Institutes of Health and the John Templeton Foundation provided support for the participation of additional institutions in the 2004 freshman survey.

*To contact: Walter R. Allen, Allan Murray Cartter Professor of Higher Education, 3101A Moore Hall, Box 951521, University of California, Los Angeles (UCLA) Graduate School of Education & Information Studies, Los Angeles, CA 90095-1521. Website: www.gseis.ucla.edu/faculty/members/allen.

"With Honors" © 1990 Synthia SAINT JAMES www.synthiasaintjames.com The original oil on canvas painting was commissioned by the House of Seagram for their "A Personal Statement" series of artwork by African American Artists which celebrated Black History Month and benefited the National Urban League.

Published by the Higher Education Research Institute. Suggested citation:
Allen, W.R., Jayakumar, U.M., Griffin, K.A., Korn, W.S., Hurtado, S. (2005). Black Undergraduates from *Bakke* to *Grutter*: Freshmen Status, Trends and Prospects, 1971–2004. Los Angeles: Higher Education Research Institute, UCLA.
Additional copies of this report can be purchased from the Higher Education Research Institute, UCLA Graduate School of Education & Information Studies, 3005 Moore Hall/Box 951521, Los Angeles, CA 90095-1521.
Please remit $15.00 plus $5.00 for shipping. Website: www.gseis.ucla.edu/heri. Telephone: 310/825-1925.

Black Undergraduates from *Bakke* to *Grutter*:

FRESHMEN STATUS, TRENDS AND PROSPECTS, 1971–2004

Contents

Tables

Figures

Foreword

The Cooperative Institutional Research Program (CIRP) is a national longitudinal study of American higher education. Established in 1966 at the American Council on Education, and transferred to the Higher Education Research Institute (HERI) at the UCLA Graduate School of Education in 1973, the CIRP is now the nation's largest and oldest empirical study of higher education, involving almost 1,800 institutions, over 11 million students, and over 350,000 faculty. Over the years, a number of studies has been generated on the experiences of underrepresented groups in higher education using CIRP data, including equity in educational attainment (Astin, 1982), campus racial climates (Hurtado, 1992), educational outcomes of diversity (Gurin, Dey, Hurtado, & Gurin, 2002; Antonio, 2004), and cross-racial interactions (Chang, Astin, & Kim, 2004; Chang, Denson, Saenz, & Misa, in press).

We commissioned this report to make use of the HERI data archives to provide information on the changing status of African Americans in higher education. This is the second report focused on Black undergraduates entering a variety of four-year colleges and universities across the nation. The first report, *The Black Undergraduate*, was written by Founding Director, Alexander Astin (1990). We are fortunate to have Walter R. Allen, an HERI-affiliated scholar who is well known for his work on Black college students in predominantly Black and predominantly White college environments, to lead this report. We hope to commission more studies focused on improving college student success in the future. As we approach the 40th year of data collection on American college students, we can say we have learned a great deal about the students' aspirations, background and preparation for college, values and attitudes, and behaviors. However, there is still much to be learned about the access and success of different types of students in different types of colleges. This report begins to fill the knowledge gap.

Sylvia Hurtado
Professor and Director
Higher Education Research Institute

BLACK UNDERGRADUATES FROM *BAKKE* TO *GRUTTER*: FRESHMEN STATUS, TRENDS AND PROSPECTS, 1971–2004

May 17, 1954 was a momentous day in American history. The U.S. Supreme Court decision in *Brown vs. Topeka Board of Education* (1954) forever changed the status of Blacks in American society. *Brown* specifically outlawed legal racial segregation against African Americans in public education. Previously Blacks were excluded from the American body public and defined as second-class citizens under the doctrine of "Separate But Equal," ensconced in constitutional law by the 1896 case *Plessy vs. Ferguson*. The implications of the *Brown* decision were far-reaching, tearing down root and branch the legal justification for an elaborately constructed system of racial subordination present in all walks of American life.

School desegregation moved at a snail's pace across the nation after the U.S. Supreme Court decision. It was not until many years later—often in the face of armed federal authority—that universities across the south finally yielded their active, determined resistance to racial integration. In September 1962, widespread rioting and two deaths resulted when U.S. troops enforced James Meridith's admission to the University of Mississippi. On June 11, 1963, Governor George Wallace stood in the schoolhouse door to physically block the integration of the University of Alabama by Vivian Malone and James Hood. He eventually stepped aside under an order from President John Kennedy and in the face of an armed presence by U.S. marshals and federal troops. It was much longer before the Black presence on campuses in the south—and across the nation—approached a critical mass. In fact, today, a half-century after the *Brown* decision, African American students still represent the slimmest token presence on the overwhelming majority of U.S. college campuses.

President Lyndon B. Johnson's affirmative action mandate attempted to address the twin heritages of slavery and Jim Crow segregation—historical and contemporary racial oppression—which kept African Americans mired in poverty and despair (Executive Order No. 11246, 1965). Issued after widespread, national racial unrest, the United States Kerner Commission report (1968) made official what everyone already knew: America continued to be a society divided by race, "separate and unequal." Johnson invoked the powerful metaphor of a people in chains for 350 years, or ten generations, being required to engage in a foot race with other people who were (and had been) free of restraints. Over the years, the unchained person of course built up quite an advantage or head start. Therefore, Johnson argued, it was not sufficient in 1965 to finally unchain African

Americans and declare the contest fair and even from that point. Johnson (1965: 2) said, "You do not take a person who, for years, has been hobbled by chains and liberate him, bring him up to the starting line of a race and then say, 'You are free to compete with all the others,' and still justly believe that you have been completely fair." After years of vigorously excluding Blacks, as well as women and other people of color, it was not enough for agencies and institutions to adopt the passive stance of "come if you want (or must)." Rather, Johnson's Executive Order called for vigorous, proactive steps—*affirmative action*—to broaden and increase access for previously excluded, underrepresented groups.

From 1965 to 1995, equal opportunity programs (and later affirmative action programs) represented rays of hope for the disenfranchised. For a relatively brief, shining moment, the doors of opportunity cracked open as never before. Blacks and others—Latinos/Latinas, women, Asians, poor Whites, the physically challenged, gays and lesbians—previously excluded from prestigious universities, corporations, and organizations slipped in, although not necessarily in massive numbers. Under the imperatives of equity, inclusiveness, and diversity, these institutions recruited African Americans and other previously excluded groups from North Carolina tobacco fields, Newark ghettos, California orchards, Oklahoma reservations, and Chicago projects. Equal opportunity and affirmative action programs gave people of color, women, and others routinely pushed to society's fringes the chance to prove their worth. These programs did not guarantee success; they merely provided the chance to compete and the opportunity to succeed (or fail).

Having proved their value and effectiveness, affirmative action programs came under withering attack. Affirmative action had made and promised further significant inroads against the established status quo of racial, patriarchal, and economic hierarchy. Predictably, powerful vested interests, under the banner of high societal ideals—colorblind society, ending "reverse discrimination," competitive testing—mounted devastating challenges to these programs. In many cases, affirmative action programs were weakened or discontinued, justified if not by unsupported claims of reverse discrimination (Pincus, 2003) then by the absurd claim that America had become a colorblind society, no longer discriminating on the basis of race (Brown et al., 2003; Omi & Winant, 1994).

Today, a full generation later, profound, dramatic changes have occurred in patterns of Black participation in U.S. higher education. Over this period, there has been a literal sea change in Black patterns and trends of college participation: There are now 1.8 million African Americans enrolled in college, fully three times the number in 1965 (Harvey & Anderson, 2005). The percentage of Black students enrolled at the University of Alabama and the University of Mississippi now exceeds by far the percentage enrolled at the University of Michigan, at the University of California at Los Angeles (UCLA) and at most other northern universities. Whereas in 1960, over three quarters of all African American college students attended Historically Black Colleges and Universities (HBCUs), by 1990, trends reversed such that more than three quarters attended Predominantly White Institutions (PWIs) (Allen, 1992). For all the gains, problems persist. Blacks continue to lag significantly behind Whites in college enrollment, graduation and advanced study (Bowen & Bok, 1998). Moreover, the national debate over the full inclusion of African Americans in institutions of higher education continues largely unabated (Chang, Witt, Jones, & Hakuta, 2003; Gurin, Lehman, Hurtado, Lewis, Dey, & Gurin, 2004; Stohr, 2004).

This report overviews the current, past and evolving status of over one-half million African American/Black[1] first-time full-time freshmen[2] in U.S. higher education since 1971, using the Cooperative Institutional Research Program (CIRP) data collected by the Higher Education Research Institute (HERI) at UCLA. As such the sample is unique, comprising the largest, most representative, longest running examination of African American first-time freshmen (and other race-ethnic groups) in existence.

BACKGROUND

While research on Black college students is extensive, very few studies provide a far-reaching overview of the characteristics of Black college students and how their profiles have changed over time. This report was commissioned to fill this gap and is the second in a series. The first report, *The Black Undergraduate*, was prepared by Alexander Astin (1990). The current report, like its predecessor, presents a national profile of contemporary African American college students and will discuss if and how these students have changed through the past three decades.

---

[1] The designation "Black" refers to both native-born and non-native-born students who self-identified as "African American/Black" on the survey.

[2] Students pursuing a full-time course of study who have had no previous college experience other than taking college courses while still in high school.

3

The Cooperative Institutional Research Program is a national normative study that documents information annually on college freshmen collected at over 600 of the country's baccalaureate colleges and universities. The surveys administered through CIRP, an endeavor of the UCLA Higher Education Research Institute, collect information on the characteristics of students entering college, demographic background, student attitudes, beliefs, values, behaviors, and future aspirations (see annual CIRP reports for copies of the surveys in each year). While our primary focus is on the general population of Black students across all institutional types, where noteworthy differences are observed, data are presented disaggregated by gender or differentiating between Black students attending historically Black colleges and universities and those attending predominantly White institutions (PWIs).

Method

During the Fall orientation or registration period of each year, the Cooperative Institutional Research Program administers a freshman survey to students enrolled in participating institutions. In 2004, 440 of the 720 participating institutions provided normative data for the national report (returning surveys from at least 75 percent of entering freshmen on each campus). Conducted since 1966, this survey reaches approximately 400,000 students annually across the United States and constitutes the oldest and largest study of higher education. Over the years, we have encouraged HBCUs to participate in the freshman survey and included them as part of our core sampling method. In 2004, particular efforts were made to involve minority-serving institutions across the country with support from foundation grants.

This report is based on the responses of 541,824 African American/Black first-time full-time freshmen attending 1,112 baccalaureate-granting colleges and universities from 1971 through 2004. Because the CIRP Freshman Survey is invitational, there may be some variation from year to year in the number of institutions of different types that choose to participate. The responses were statistically weighted to estimate the national population of first-time full-time Black freshmen during that period (approximately 3.6 million). The weighting procedure is designed to compensate for over- and under-sampling of institutional participants in 26 "Stratification Cells" based on their control (public, private, etc.), type (four-year college or university) and selectivity (the average SAT Composite score for the entering class). A detailed description of the stratification and weighting procedures used for this study can be found in Appendix A of *The American Freshman: National Norms for Fall, 2004* (Sax, Hurtado, Lindholm, Astin, Korn, & Mahoney, 2004).

A student's responses were included in this report if he/she marked "African American/Black" to the ethnicity question on the CIRP survey. It should be noted that this question allows students to mark as many of the ethnic categories as are applicable. We chose to include students even though they may have marked other ethnic groups in addition to "African American/Black." We have observed that the percentage of students marking more than one ethnic group has risen steadily since the inception of the survey in 1966. It is also important to note that the terms "African American" and "Black" are used interchangeably in this report because students marked this racial identification category, though we know that approximately 3.7 percent were not American-born Blacks.

OVERVIEW OF THE REPORT

The following pages present normative data on Black freshmen who began their college journey between 1971 to 2004. Results cover a wide variety of characteristics of these freshmen. After a brief overview of the social and institutional context for educating Black students, results are presented under selected categories: family socioeconomic status, academic background and aspirations, college choice, financial aid, and political and civic engagement. Interested readers may find it helpful to compare this report to *The American Freshman: National Norms*, which details results from the total sample of American first-year undergraduates surveyed in 2004 (Sax et al., 2004). While more detail is provided in this section, the tables at the end of the report show an overview of changes among Black freshmen in the 1970s (using different years sometimes as starting points) as compared with students in 2004.

The Cooperative Institutional Research Program data files represent an amazing and unique repository, chronicling the history of U.S. higher education over the past thirty years. This period has arguably been the most significant in the history of American higher education; certainly, this is true with respect to the changes that have occurred driven by the engines of social protest. The Civil Rights Movement and various other social movements laid the foundation and provided the backdrop for these dramatic changes (Morris, 1984). The diverse face of U.S. higher education today reflects the accomplished goals of these movements that pushed for expanded access, diversity and equity. At the same time, we see in sharp relief the challenges that remain for African Americans, Latinos, the poor and others as they strive to achieve access and success in U.S. higher education.

BLACK UNDERGRADUATES AT BACCALAUREATE-GRANTING INSTITUTIONS IN THE U.S.

Women are a sizeable majority among all African American freshman undergraduates surveyed, and the gender gap widened over time (Figure 1). In 1971, women comprised 55 percent of the overall sample, but this percentage had increased to 59 percent by 2004. While other race-ethnic groups have recently discovered a gender gap in college participation, the pattern where women enroll in college at higher rates has been a long-established pattern among African Americans. Yet, the trend indicates that the gap continues to grow steadily, portending lower college attainment rates for Black males. This is further evidenced in a widening of the gender gap on achievement, aspirations, attitudes, and behaviors that are noted throughout this report.

Other ongoing changes and debates from the larger society are also reflected in these data on African American freshman undergraduates. For instance, immigration has changed the face of America dramatically since the 1970s and we also see a marginal increase in freshmen who identify as Black but are not American-born. Between 1972 and 2004, the fraction of Black freshman

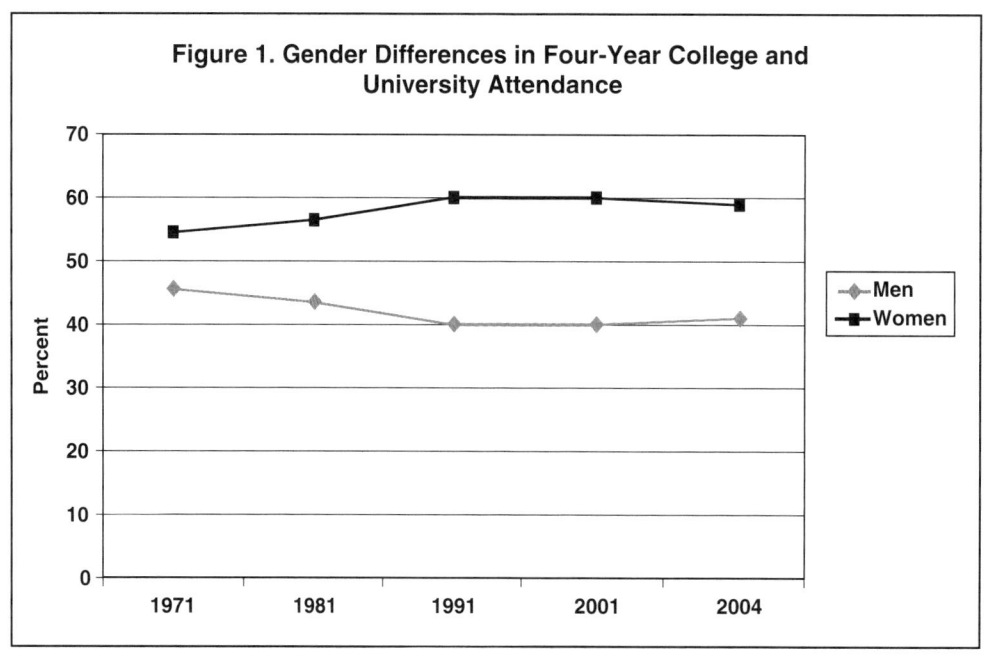

students who were not American citizens grew from 3 percent to nearly 4 percent. In 2004, these students were more likely to be found at predominantly White institutions (5 percent) as opposed to HBCUs (2 percent).

In similar fashion—and to no one's surprise—African American college freshmen were not untouched by resurgent and changing religious interests over the last thirty years. We noted significant shifts within the category of students who self-identified as Protestants. Historically, African Americans have been disproportionately Baptist in religious affiliation, likely owing to the community's earliest connections with largely Baptist, White populations in rural, southern, working-class and poor areas (Morris, 1984). In 2004, 44 percent of Black freshmen self-identified as Baptist, down from 51 percent in 1973. Despite this decrease, Black students were still considerably more likely than students in the general freshman population to indicate that they were Baptist (44 percent vs. 12 percent in 2004). The next largest religious category among Black freshmen in 2004 was "other Christian" (Protestant) at 22 percent, up from 3 percent in 1973. Smaller numbers listed Roman Catholic (7 percent), "other religion" (4 percent) or no religion (10 percent).

FAMILY SOCIOECONOMIC STATUS

In general there was an upward trend in socioeconomic status among African American freshman undergraduates in terms of standard measures of income and education. It is fair to say that the first-generation, lower-income Black freshmen of the '70s were quite distinct from the better positioned, more affluent cohorts who entered college in later years (Figures 2 and 3). In 1971, 41 percent of first-year African American students reported they were from a low-income family[3] (less than $6,000 per year), contrasting with the 30 percent who indicated their families were low-income in 2004 (less than $25,000 annually). The differences at the upper end of the income spectrum are more pronounced, with only 2 percent of respondents reporting family incomes of $30,000 or higher in 1971 compared to 13 percent claiming annual family earnings above $100,000 in 2004. Despite significant gains and increases in the number of Black students

---

[3]For the purposes of this report, low-income families do not have incomes in excess of 150% of the federally defined poverty level for a family of four for that given year. Poverty thresholds for 1950–2002 were obtained from Social Security Online (http://www.ssa.gov/policy/docs/statcomps/supplement/2003/3e.html) and 2004 data was obtained from the United States Department of Health and Human Services (http://aspe.hhs.gov/poverty/figures-fed-reg.shtml). The federal poverty levels for families of four in 1971 and 2004 were $4,137 and $18,850, respectively.

from families earning $100,000 per year, they still lag behind the largely White, general student population, 32 percent of which reported this income level.

In the early '70s, roughly equal proportions of affluent Black students attended HBCUs and predominantly White institutions (2 percent vs. 1 percent of students reporting incomes over $30,000). Similarly in 2004, comparable percentages of students in the highest income categories attended PWIs and HBCUs (14 percent vs. 12 percent of Black students reporting incomes over $100,000). However, at both time points, a larger percentage of Black freshmen at HBCUs were from low-income families (43 percent in 1971 and 34 percent in 2004) than at PWIs (39 percent in 1971 and 28 percent in 2004). Male students appeared to come from more affluent backgrounds than their female counterparts. While this trend was observed among students at HBCUs (14 percent men vs. 10 percent women in 2004), this difference was slightly more pronounced at PWIs (17 percent men vs. 12 percent women).

Of course, these earnings figures should be adjusted to take account of rising wages and inflation; nevertheless, the sheer scale of difference in representation in the lowest and highest annual family income categories among first-year Black college students over these three decades is noteworthy. Adjustments to constant dollars aside, there has been a dramatic shift upward in the family economic status of entering African American undergraduates.

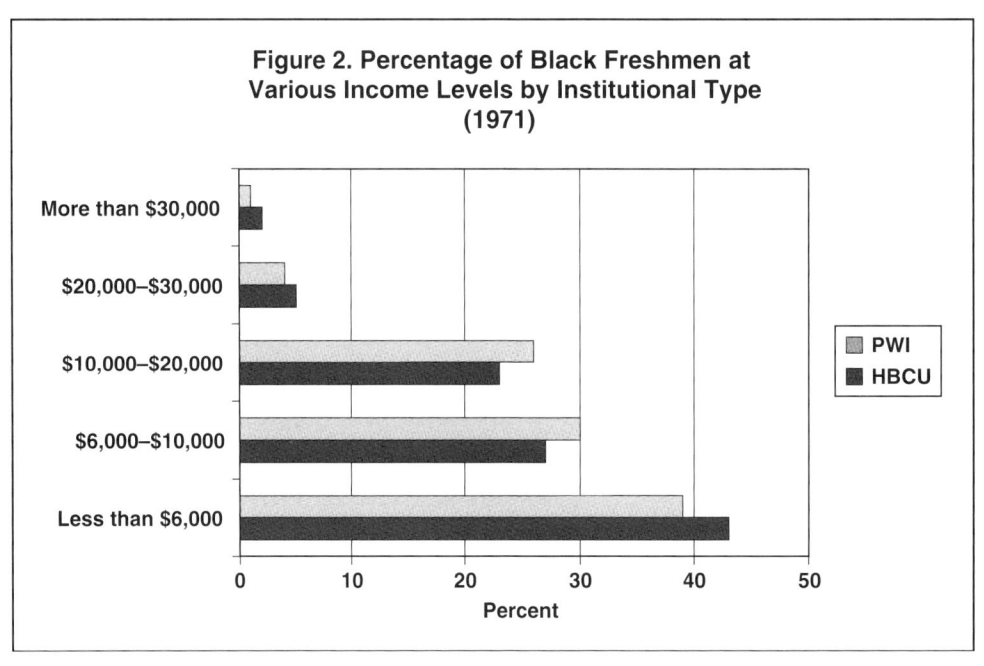

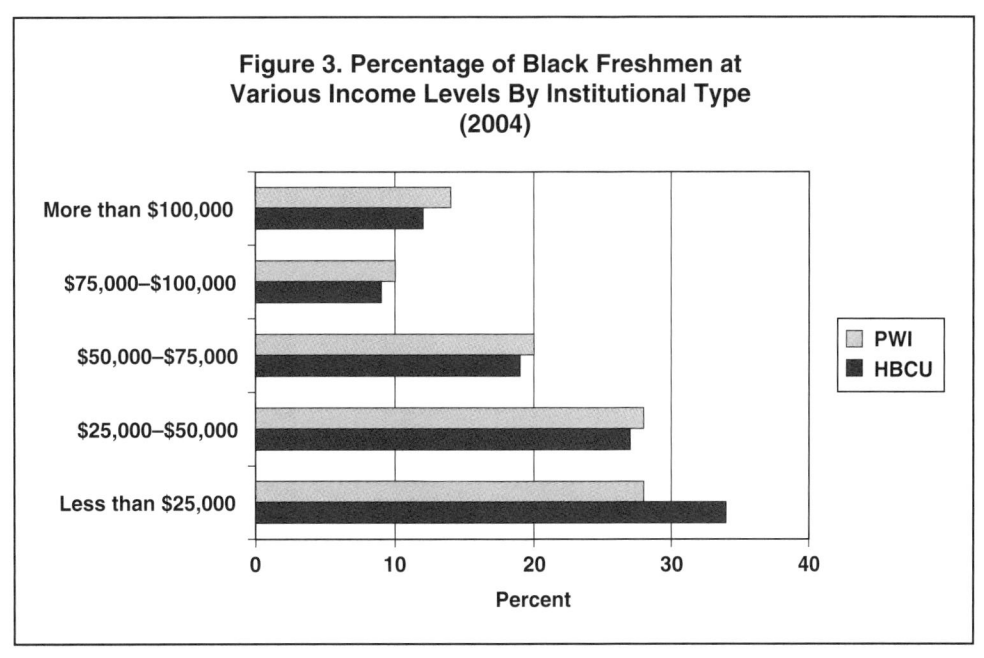

Figure 3. Percentage of Black Freshmen at Various Income Levels By Institutional Type (2004)

We see similar improvements in parents' educational attainment reported by Black freshmen from 1971 to 2004. On balance, the general patterns and trends indicate that the parents of African American 2004 freshmen had significantly higher educational attainment than the parents of 1971 African American first-year students (Figure 4). Specifically, for the 1971 cohort, 11 percent of fathers and 14 percent of mothers had some college; 8 percent of fathers and 11 percent of mothers were college graduates; and 5 percent of both mothers and fathers earned graduate degrees. For the 2004 African American freshman cohort, 19 percent of fathers and 24 percent of mothers had some college; 20 percent of fathers and 25 percent of mothers were college graduates; and 13 percent of fathers and 14 percent of mothers had graduate degrees. There were also some remarkable differences by institutional type. In 1971, students at HBCUs reported having somewhat better educated parents (15 percent fathers, 18 percent mothers with a college degree or higher) than those at PWIs (13 percent for both fathers and mothers with a college degree or higher). By 2004, the trend reversed: Students at PWIs reported having better educated parents, specifically fathers (36 percent of fathers, 41 percent of mothers with a college degree or beyond), than those at HBCUs (30 percent of fathers, 40 percent of mothers with a college degree or beyond). When comparing Black students' parent education levels with the general freshman population, we can see that Black parents continue to have relatively less formal education. Among all freshmen in 2004, 53 percent of fathers and 52 percent of mothers had at least a college degree.

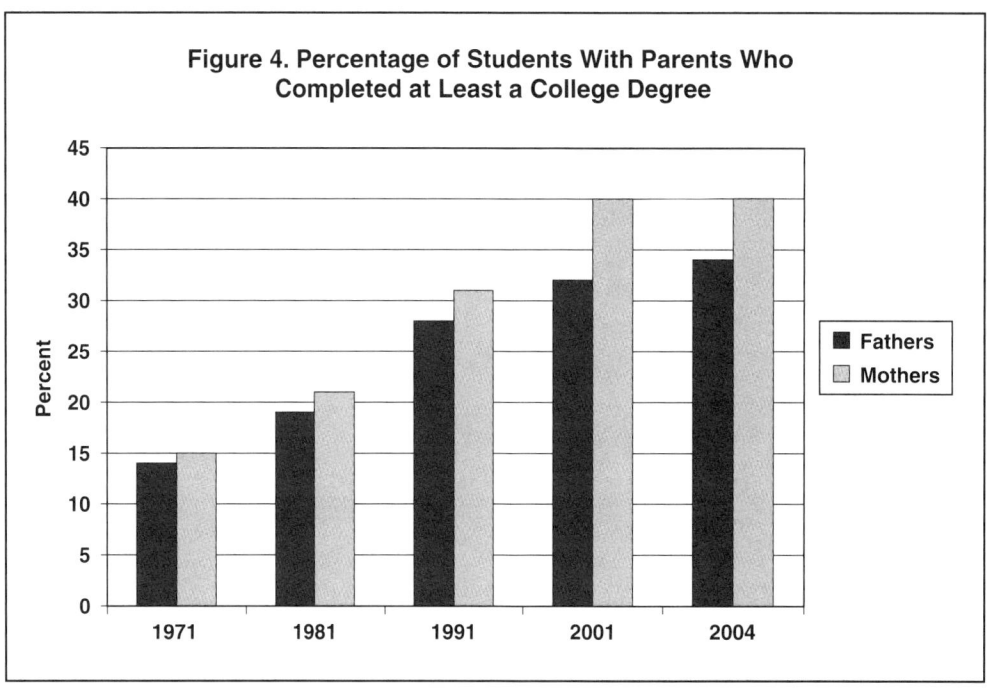

Figure 4. Percentage of Students With Parents Who Completed at Least a College Degree

Parent occupations also showed evidence of important change over the thirty-year period (Figure 5). In 1971, the fathers of African American freshmen were concentrated in blue-collar positions: 13 percent skilled trades, 15 percent unskilled laborers, and 16 percent semi-skilled workers. A sizeable 35 percent of mothers were full-time homemakers. Of mothers employed outside the home, 11 percent worked as elementary or secondary school teachers or administrators. By 2004, these patterns shifted in significant ways as fewer fathers worked as laborers: 8 percent skilled trades, 4 percent unskilled laborers, and 4 percent semi-skilled laborers. More fathers were employed as business executives (7 vs. 3 percent) or were business owners or proprietors (5 vs. 3 percent). There was also considerable growth in the numbers of mothers employed in business to 17 percent, breaking down as clerical workers (5 percent), executives (7 percent), owners or proprietors (3 percent), and salespersons or buyers (2 percent). The largest single occupational category for mothers of 2004 Black freshmen was business (17 vs. 3 percent), followed by nursing (11 vs. 7 percent). The percentage of mothers working as elementary and secondary school teachers or administrators remained at 11 percent across both time points.

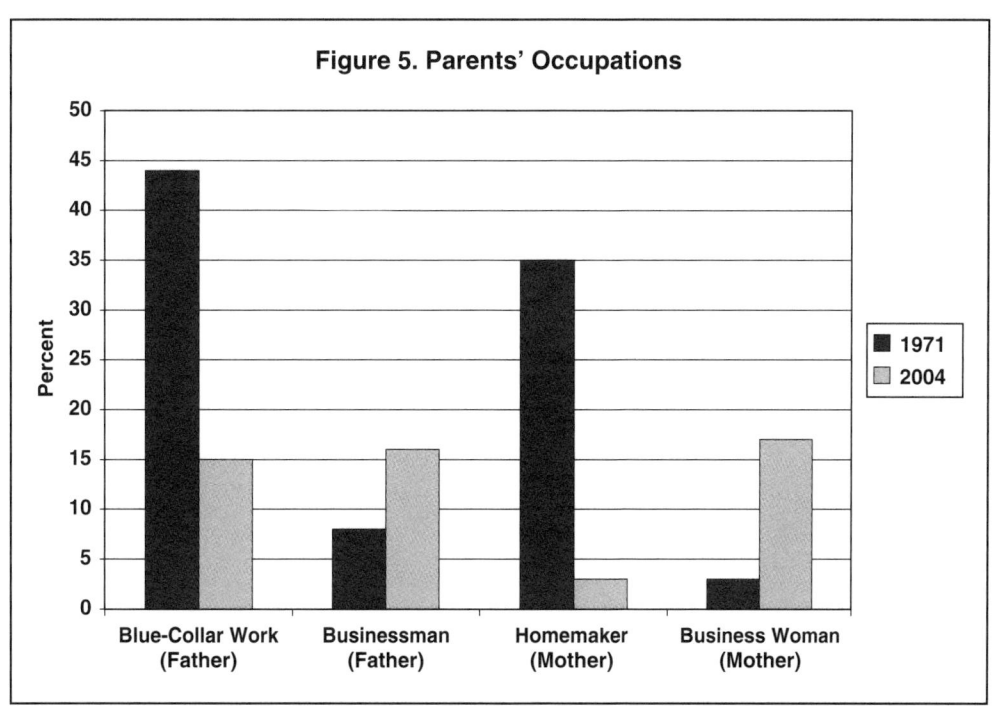

Figure 5. Parents' Occupations

Taken together, thirty-year increases in the family socioeconomic status of African American freshmen reveal more about dramatic shifts among the particular Black students who enroll in college and perhaps less about relative improvements in the overall economic status of Blacks in this society. There is abundant evidence confirming persistent economic disadvantage by race in America, revealed most powerfully in the growing chasm between "haves" and "have-nots" within the African American community (Brown et al., 2003). This economic schism reflects a parallel pattern and set of problems evident in the larger society.

FINANCIAL NEED

In 2004, 26 percent of Black students had no concerns about financing their college education, but in 1971, 18 percent reported they had no concerns. Perhaps connected to increases in family income, Black students' expressing major concerns over ability to finance college decreased from 26 percent to 23 percent between 1971 and 2004. However, Black students were still more concerned today about financing their college education than their peers (23 percent of Black students vs. 13 percent of all freshmen had major concerns). While more certain that they would be able to finance their education, African American freshmen were increasingly likely to anticipate

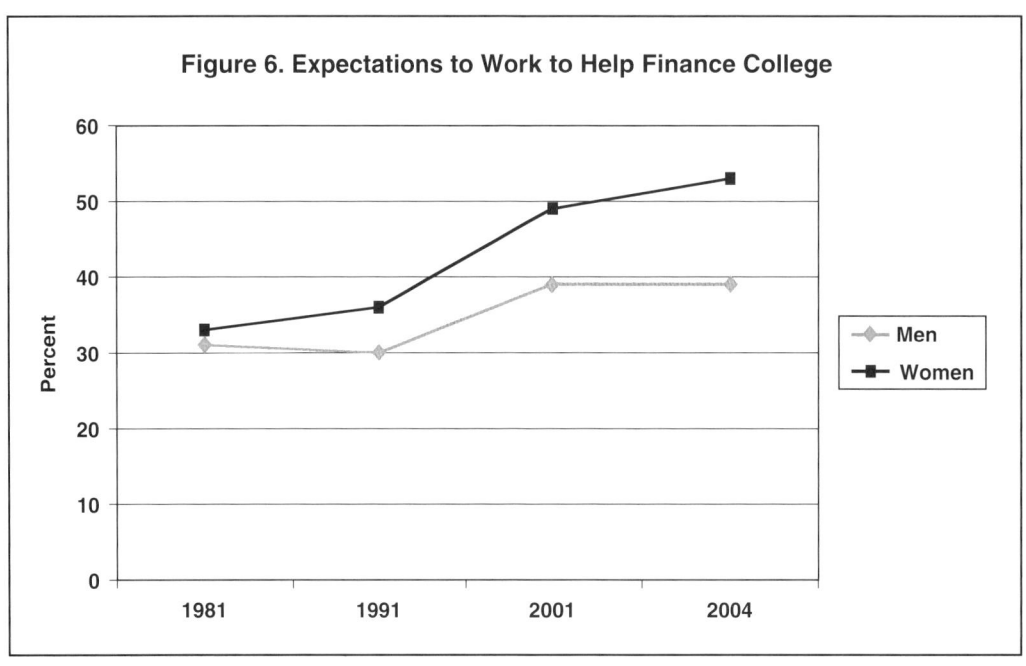

Figure 6. Expectations to Work to Help Finance College

working to help pay for college expenses (Figure 6). When first measured in 1976, 27 percent of Black students thought they would need to get a job to help pay for college, which increased to 47 percent of students by 2004. In 2004, women were more likely than men to expect to have a job (53 vs. 39 percent). Intentions to work full-time while in college increased from 5 percent to 9 percent between 1982 and 2004. In 2004, women were more likely to expect to work full-time during college than their male counterparts (10 vs. 7 percent).

Today's Black undergraduates are more likely to rely on various forms of financial aid to cover college costs (Figure 7). Loans were more frequently utilized by students overall and, between 1981 and 2000, the percentage of Black freshmen taking college loans (e.g., Stafford, Perkins, and other) in excess of $1,500 grew from 16 percent to 46 percent. In 1981, 17 percent of students received $1,500 or more from Pell grants; the percentage grew slightly to 21 percent by 2000. With the emergence of numerous state-based merit aid programs in the 1990s, it is not surprising to see increases in the number of Black undergraduates receiving state scholarships between 1981 (3 percent) and 2000 (13 percent). In 1981, a comparable percentage of males and females received state awards greater than $1,500 (4 percent vs. 3 percent, respectively) and the numbers across gender remained comparable through 2000, with 14 percent of women and 12 percent of men receiving state scholarships.

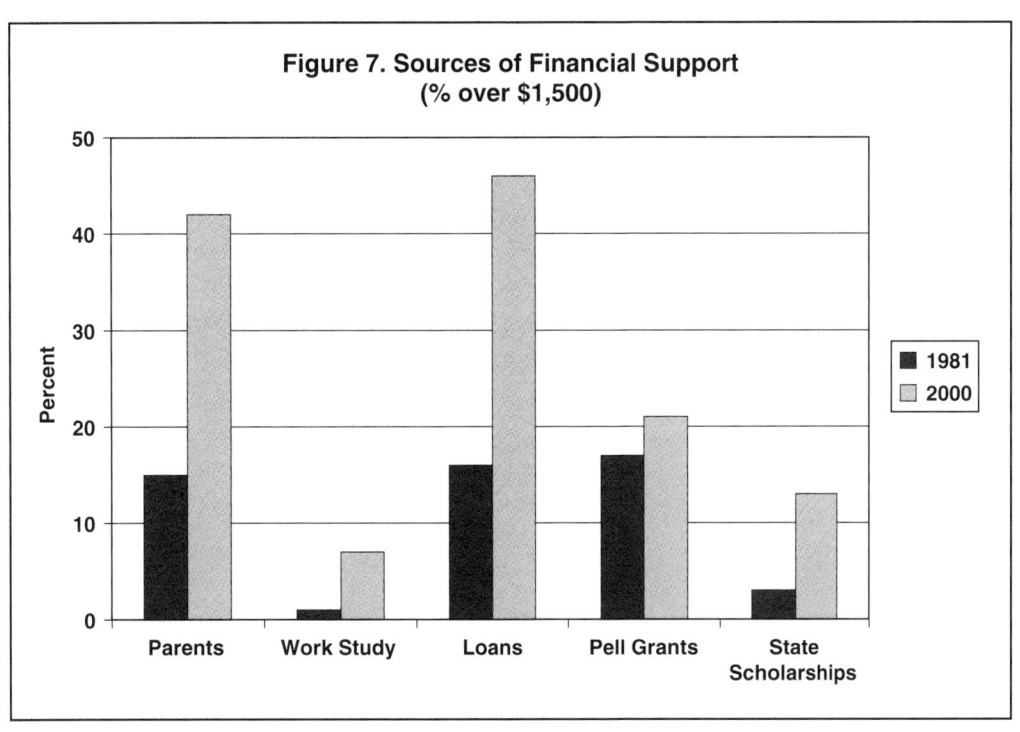

Figure 7. Sources of Financial Support
(% over $1,500)

ACADEMIC BACKGROUND AND ASPIRATIONS

Comparisons of the 1971 and 2004 cohorts of African American freshmen also reveal significant upward trends in overall academic preparation and aspirations. For instance in 1971, 8 percent of Black freshmen reported high school grade point averages of "A–" or better compared to 20 percent of freshmen overall; by 2004, 28 percent of Black freshmen were in this range. Despite significant increases, Black students' achievement was still lower. In 2004, a significantly higher percentage (48 percent) of the general population reported "A" averages in high school. Students at PWIs were more likely to have an "A" average entering college than students at HBCUs over all time points, and Black women were significantly more likely to have "A" averages at both institutional types. In 2004, 33 percent of women and 20 percent of men reported "A–" or better averages.

Overall, there were dramatic rising trends in self-ratings by African American freshmen from 1971 to 2004. In each instance, the 2004 cohort were considerably more likely than their 1971 counterparts to rate themselves above average or in the top 10 percent on each attribute: academic ability (62 vs. 33 percent), artistic ability (30 vs. 14 percent), drive to achieve (79 vs. 63 percent), leadership (66 vs. 38 percent), mathematical ability (37 vs. 19 percent), writing ability (47 vs. 28 percent) and predictably, intellectual self-confidence (69 vs. 39 percent). Compared to the national freshman student population, Black freshmen in 2004 appeared less confident about their overall academic ability (62 vs. 70 percent) and mathematical ability (37 vs. 45 percent). However, Black students were more likely to rate themselves above average or in the top 10 percent regarding drive to achieve (79 vs. 71 percent), leadership ability (66 vs. 60 percent), and intellectual self-confidence (69 vs. 58 percent). While self-ratings were fairly similar across institutional types, Black students at PWIs expressed greater confidence in their abilities than students entering HBCUs. For example, 58 percent of HBCU freshmen and 65 percent of PWI freshmen rated themselves above average or in the top 10 percent in academic ability. However, research indicates that upon graduation, students at HBCUs have significantly higher self-ratings, retention rates, and academic aspirations than their counterparts at PWIs (Allen, 1992). The fact that students at PWIs start off higher but graduate with lower academic self-confidence likely speaks to differences in academic experiences and campus climates. For example, PWIs have been shown to be more hostile and less supportive (Allen, 1992). Also, despite superior academic performance and greater time spent studying and doing homework in high school, women felt less confident about their academic abilities than men (Figure 8). The data indicated that men rated themselves more highly than women in terms of their academic ability (64 vs. 61 percent), leadership ability (69 vs. 65 percent), and intellectual self-confidence (76 vs. 65 percent). Certainly, differences in societal gender-role expectations and

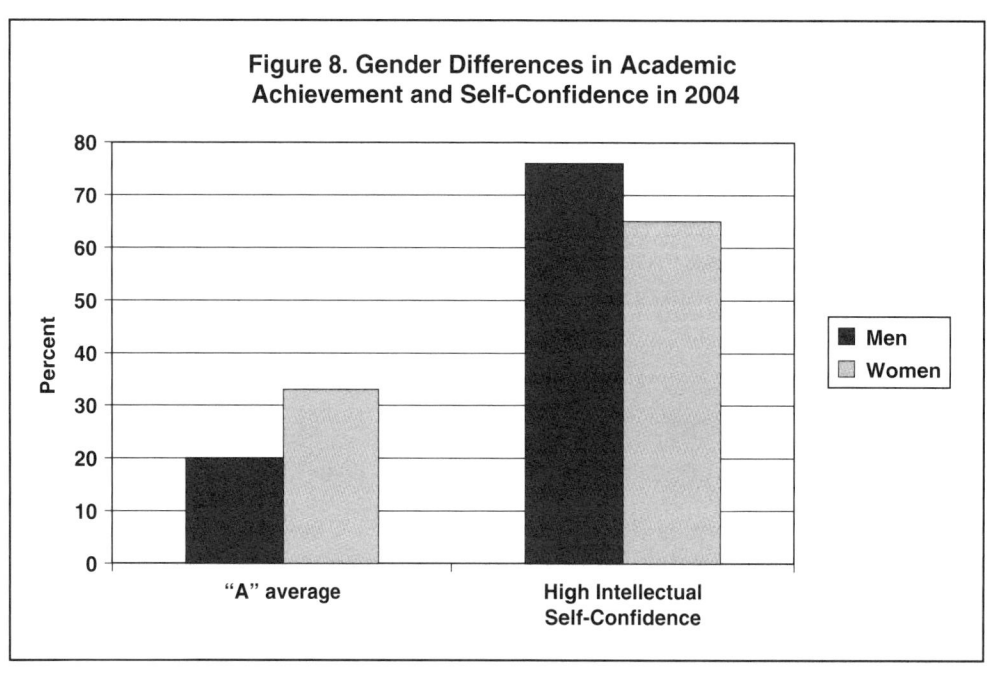

14

gender disparities in educational experiences help to explain declines in women's academic aspirations and performance over time (Fleming, 1984; Holland, 1990).

Between 1971 and 2003, there were substantial decreases in Black first-year college students who felt they needed special tutoring or remedial work in English (22 percent in 1971 vs. 16 percent in 2003), reading (13 vs. 7 percent), mathematics (56 vs. 44 percent), science (30 vs. 21 percent) and foreign language (36 vs. 21 percent). In addition, there were substantial gains between 1984 and 2004 in the numbers of Black freshmen who met or exceeded the minimum recommendations of the National Commission on Excellence in Education (1983) in terms of years of study in English (4 years), 93 percent in 1984 to 97 percent in 2004; mathematics (3 years), 83 to 97 percent; and foreign language (2 years), 60 to 89 percent. Regarding curricular preparation, these increases brought Black students to near parity with the general pool of entering freshmen in 2004. However, more research is needed concerning the types of courses students have access to in high school: Black students were still less likely to meet or exceed the recommended two years of foreign language (89 vs. 92 percent) or physical science (45 vs. 59 percent) than the general freshman population. Persistent disparities in academic preparation for college reflect the extreme disadvantages of the primary and secondary schools Black students attend (e.g., fewer educational resources, less experienced teachers, more limited course offerings) (Kozol, 2005; Oakes, Mendoza, & Silver, 2004).

In 1971, African American freshmen mentioned a wider range of probable college majors (Table 1), with the largest categories being general business administration (10 percent), general education (8 percent), psychology (6 percent), medical/dental/veterinary (5 percent), sociology (5 percent), and nursing (4 percent). By 2004, probable majors for Black freshmen were more concentrated. Twelve percent specified business: general administration (4 percent), management (5 percent) and accounting (3 percent). Seven percent of this cohort chose general biology as a probable college major, 7 percent named psychology, and 4 percent selected elementary education. Notably, the percentages of Black students anticipating majoring in biology and business were higher than the percentages of students interested in these majors in the general student population in 2004, but Black students tended to express less interest in education than the average student (7 vs. 10 percent).

Table 1. The Top Ten Major Fields for Black Freshmen in 1971 and 2004

1971	%	2004	%
Business Administration (general)	10	Biology (general)	7
General Education	8	Psychology	7
Psychology	6	Nursing	6
Medical, Dental, Veterinary	5	Medical, Dental, Veterinary	6
Sociology	5	Management	5
Nursing	4	Business Administration (general)	4
Social Work	4	Elementary Education	4
Physical Education or Recreation	4	Political Science	3
Accounting	4	Marketing	3
History	3	Accounting	3

NOTE: The responses "Other" and "Undecided" were not included although they were among the top ten responses in each year.

Associated with the observed trends of enhanced academic preparation were higher educational and occupational aspirations. In 1971, 28 percent of African American freshmen aspired to Bachelor's degrees (B.A., B.S., etc.), 37 percent to Master's degrees (M.A., M.S., etc.), 17 percent to doctoral degrees (Ph.D. or Ed.D.), 7 percent to medical degrees (M.D., D.D.S., D.V.M. or D.O.), and 6 percent to law degrees (LL.B. or J.D.). By 2004, there was an upward shift such that 17 percent aspired to Bachelor's degrees, 36 percent to Master's degrees, 24 percent to doctoral degrees, 12 percent to medical degrees, and 6 percent to law degrees. Consistent with previous research on Black students' degree and educational aspirations (Bowen & Bok, 1998), they also tended to have higher degree aspirations than the average freshman in 2004. Twenty-four percent of Black students intended to obtain a Ph.D. or Ed.D., as compared to 17 percent of the general population of students, and Black students were slightly more likely to express interest in professional degrees—medical degrees (12 vs. 9 percent) and law degrees (6 vs. 5 percent). In 2004, Black women were twice as likely (16 percent) to aspire toward medical degrees than were men (8 percent). This gender difference is considerably more pronounced among Black students than for the general student population, where only four percentage points separate women and men (11 vs. 7 percent) interested in attaining medical degrees.

Interesting shifts were also observed in the career aspirations of African American freshmen over this period (Table 2). In 1971, 17 percent aspired to careers as elementary (8 percent) or secondary (9 percent) schoolteachers or administrators, 5 percent as physicians, 7 percent attorneys, 9 percent business executives, 4 percent engineers, and 8 percent social workers. By 2004, there had been major changes in overall career aspirations: Only 6 percent of Black freshmen aspired to be K–12 teachers or administrators (3 percent in the elementary area and 3 percent in secondary school), 10 percent aspired to become physicians, 8 percent business executives and, respectively, 6 percent lawyers, engineers or nurses. From 1971 to 2004, pronounced patterns of change in career aspirations are observed (Figure 9). The proportions of Black freshmen who aspired to be K–12 teachers or administrators dropped precipitously, declining more than half, as did those who aspired to become social workers (down by 85 percent). On the other hand, the percentage who aspired to become physicians doubled over this time period.

Table 2. The Top Ten Career Aspirations for Black Freshmen in 1971 and 2004

1971	%	2004	%
Business executive (mgmt., admin.)	9	Physician	10
Teacher or administrator (secondary)	9	Business executive (mgmt., admin.)	8
Social welfare or recreation worker	8	Nurse	6
Teacher or administrator (elementary)	8	Engineer	6
Lawyer (attorney) or judge	7	Lawyer (attorney) or judge	6
Physician	5	Business owner or proprietor	4
Engineer	4	Computer programmer or analyst	4
Nurse	4	Teacher or administrator (elementary and secondary)	6
Accountant or actuary	4	Pharmacist	3
Business (clerical)	3	Accountant or actuary	3

NOTE: The responses "Other" and "Undecided" were not included although they were among the top ten responses in each year.

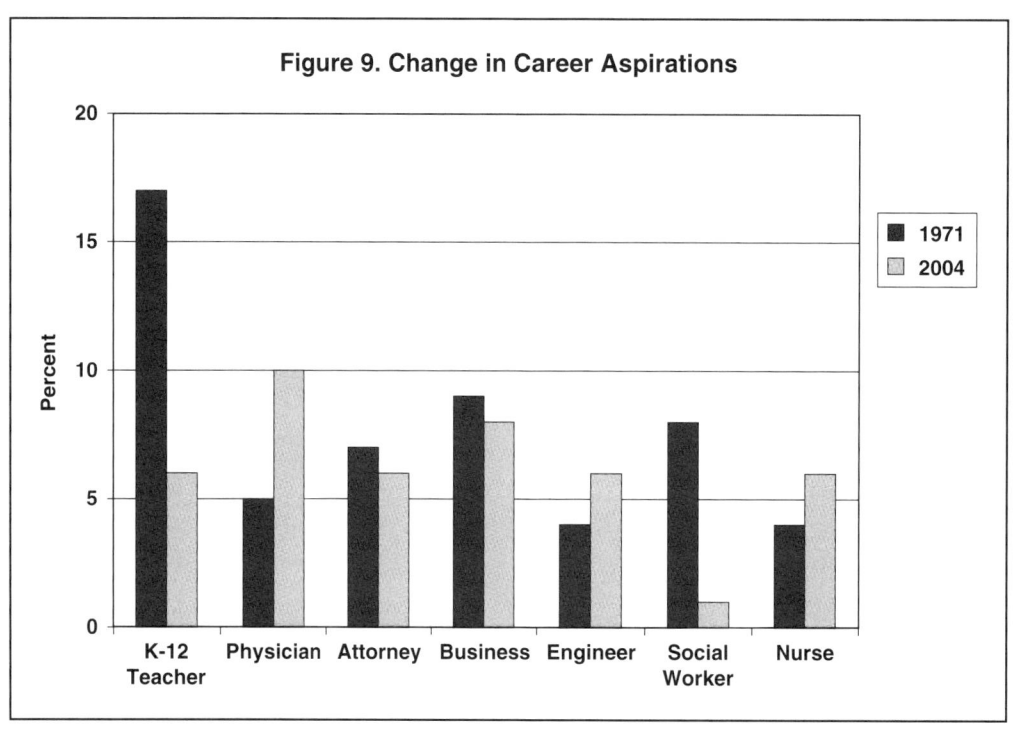

Figure 9. Change in Career Aspirations

COLLEGE CHOICE

For Black freshmen, the most compelling reasons for attending college across time have been upward mobility and a desire to acquire a greater knowledge base. An overwhelming and growing majority of Black students (at both HBCUs and PWIs) place great importance on the goal of being very well-off financially, at least 80 percent every year since 1982. Indeed, the undergraduate degree has increasingly become a means to attaining graduate or professional degrees (56 percent in 1971 to 69 percent in 2004), rather than an end in and of itself. By 2004, Black students were much more likely to attend college to prepare for graduate school than freshmen overall (69 percent vs. 57 percent). Among the reasons noted by students for going to college in 2004 were: to get a better job (77 percent), have greater earning potential (82 percent), and learn more about things that interest them (78 percent). By comparison, the top three reasons cited for going to college by the general group of freshmen entering college in 2004 were: to learn more about things of interest (77 percent), get training for a specific career (75 percent), and get a better job (72 percent). African American students' understanding of the importance of higher education for economic advancement perhaps derives from parents and mentors, who play central roles in shaping their orientation toward college. In 2004, half of the Black students (50 percent) indicated that their parents were influential in the development of their college aspirations.

Financial aid was one of the more influential factors affecting students' college attendance decisions (Figure 10). Across all time points, between 39 and 48 percent of Black freshmen indicated that financial assistance was a "very important" influence on the decision to attend a particular college. For Black freshmen in 2004, other factors considered in choosing to attend a particular college included academic reputation (59 percent), reputation for its social activities (30 percent), job market success of the college's graduates (54 percent), and the advantages the institution provided students who applied to graduate/professional schools (37 percent).

While the reasons indicated as important in choosing a particular college suggest well informed decision making, it is sometimes unclear how these students are obtaining their information. It appears that students are not acquiring knowledge about colleges from school agents, who are best positioned to provide such information. High school guidance counselors influenced college choice for only 11 percent of the students in 2004. Seven percent of Black students felt that the advice of teachers was a very important factor in their decision and 10 percent responded to an offer from college recruiters (in 1997, when last recorded). The minimal role of school counselors and teachers in the college choice process for Black students is particularly troubling given the profound role these school agents play in setting expectations around college-going (McDonough,

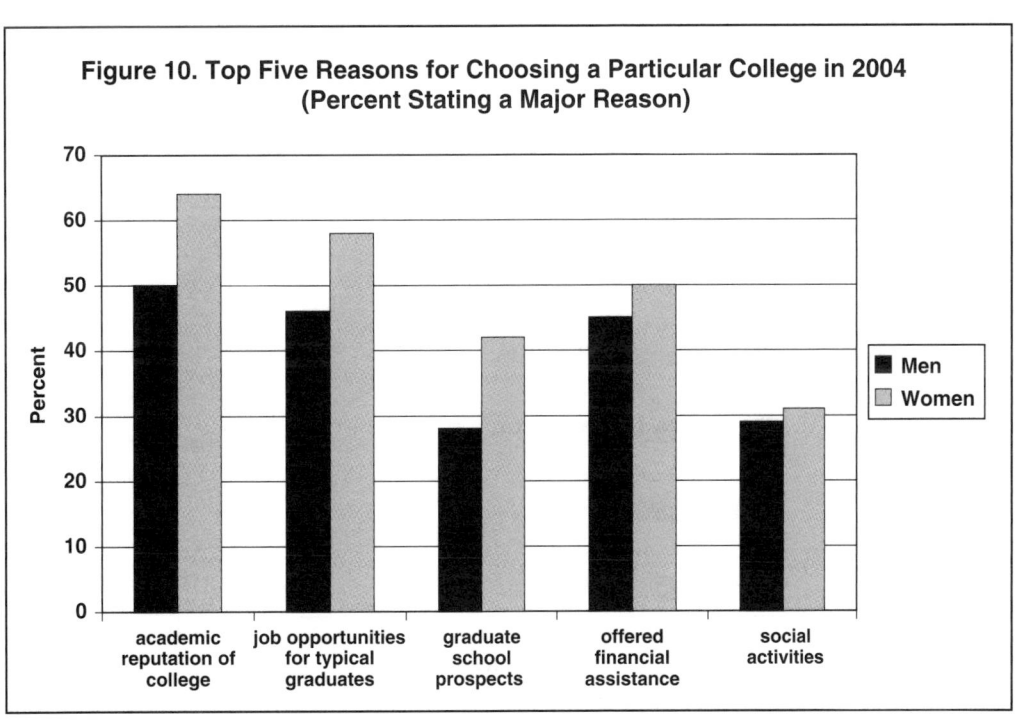

Figure 10. Top Five Reasons for Choosing a Particular College in 2004 (Percent Stating a Major Reason)

1998; Stanton-Salazar, 2001). Interestingly, Black students were still more likely than the average freshman to turn to teachers and counselors for information: 5 percent of 2004 freshmen reported that teachers impacted their college choice and 7 percent indicated high school counselors.

For the 2004 Black undergraduates under study, college choice information sources varied by institutional type and included college ranking magazines (22 percent at HBCUs and 17 percent at PWIs), relatives (17 percent at HBCUs and 12 percent at PWIs), and friends (10 percent at HBCUs and 9 percent at PWIs). There were also important gender differences in college information sources (Figure 11). Men more often cited friends, relatives, college recruiters and teachers as key sources. By contrast, women more often cited written materials such as college ranking magazines.

Previous research found proximity to home to be among the top reasons African American students chose PWIs over HBCUs (McDonough, Antonio, & Trent, 1997), and some differences across institutional types did emerge in this analysis. It appears that a larger percentage of Black freshmen at PWIs took distance from home into account in making their college choice. Seventeen percent of students at HBCUs and 21 percent at PWIs rated staying close to home as an important reason for choosing their particular college.

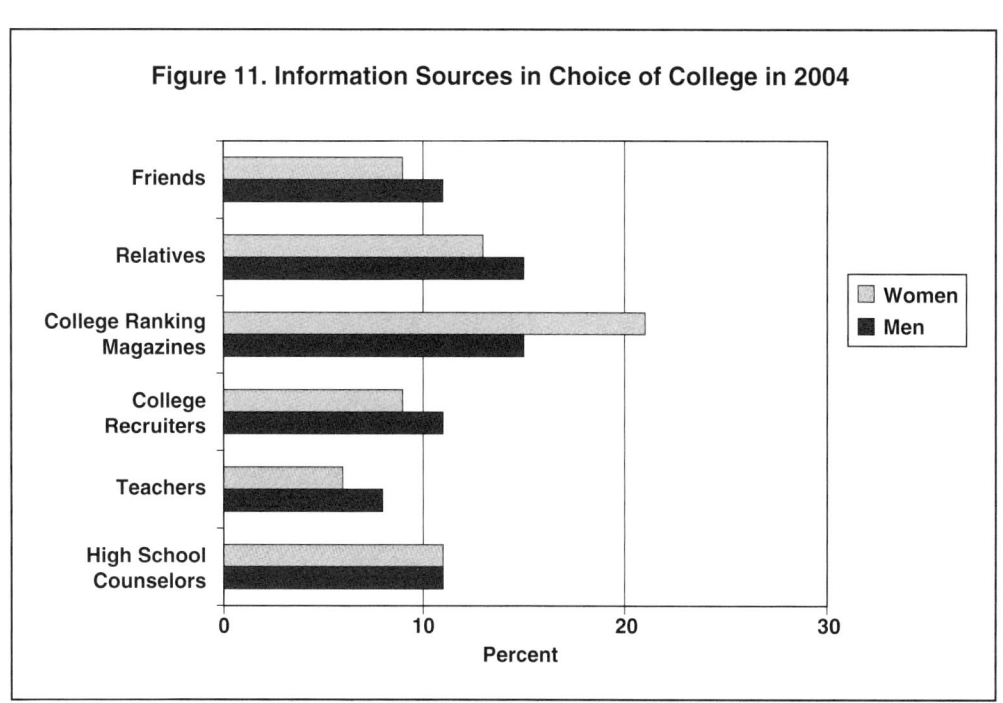

GRADUATE SCHOOL

Several indicators revealed a stronger graduate school orientation among Black women. For example, women on average were more likely to view college as preparation for graduate school (80 percent of women at HBCUs and 75 percent at PWIs compared to 61 percent of men at HBCUs and 55 percent at PWIs). Indeed, in deciding on a particular institution, women placed greater importance on graduate school prospects (45 percent women vs. 29 percent men at HBCUs; 41 percent vs. 28 percent at PWIs), the academic reputation of the college (64 percent women vs. 46 percent men at HBCUs; 65 percent vs. 52 percent at PWIs), and job opportunities for typical graduates (60 percent women vs. 45 percent men at HBCUs; 58 percent vs. 47 percent at PWIs). They were also more likely to consult college ranking magazines than men (27 percent women vs. 15 percent men at HBCUs; 17 percent vs. 16 percent at PWIs). While women seemed to give greater forethought than men to how choice of undergraduate institution fits into graduate school planning, men's stated aspirations to attain a doctoral degree (21 percent) were close to the percentage for women (26 percent). It would appear that while both men and women had high educational aspirations, women seemed to have a clearer sense of the necessary steps to reach their stated graduate school goals. These data have implications for outreach and other programming targeted at increasing African American student enrollment in graduate and professional schools. For example, women may need greater exposure to successful role models and confidence-building activities while it may be more critical for men to receive information and encouragement on the specific intermediate steps necessary to achieve their goals.

POLITICAL AND CIVIC ENGAGEMENT

Reflecting a general trend in students' political affiliations since 1971 (Astin, Oseguera, Sax, & Korn, 2002), Black freshmen appeared to be less liberal and more likely to identify themselves as moderate or conservative across the years (Figures 12 and 13). Approximately 50 percent of Black freshmen reported that they were "liberal" or "far left" in 1971; by 2004, the percentage had decreased to 36 percent. Black students were still more likely to identify as far left or liberal than the general freshman population; in 2004, 30 percent of freshmen overall so identified themselves. While Black men appeared to be more liberal or far left in 1971 (52 percent of men vs. 48 percent of women), this trend reversed by the early 1980s and thereafter, Black women appeared to have a

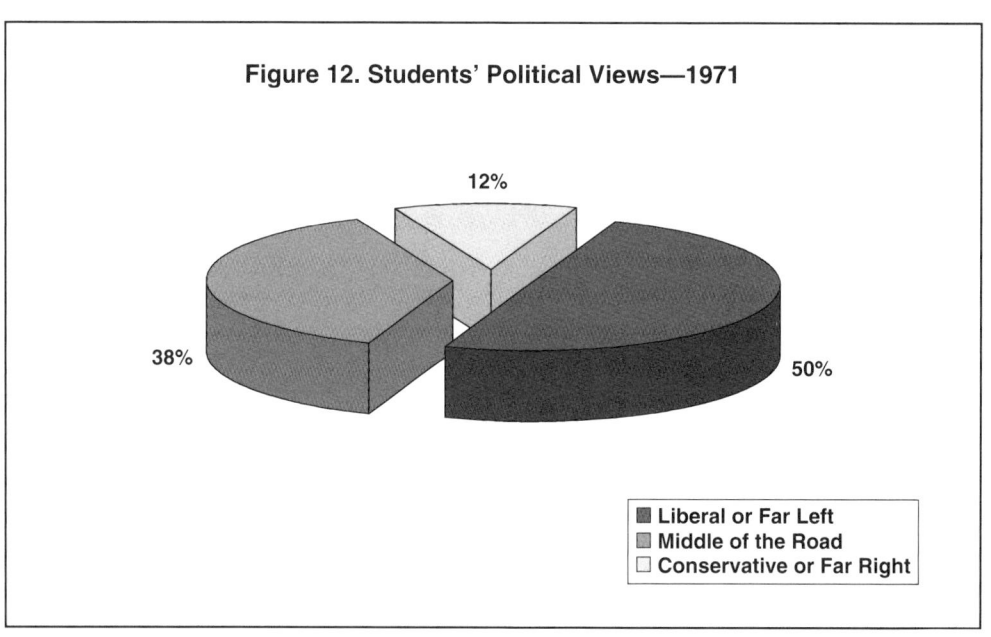

Figure 12. Students' Political Views—1971

12%

38%

50%

Liberal or Far Left
Middle of the Road
Conservative or Far Right

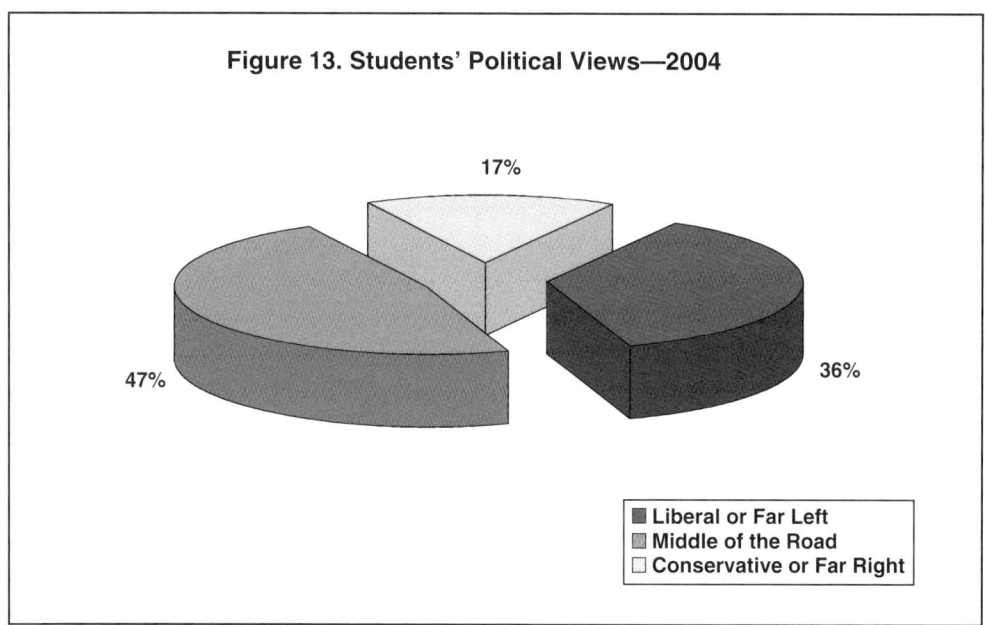

Figure 13. Students' Political Views—2004

17%

47%

36%

Liberal or Far Left
Middle of the Road
Conservative or Far Right

more liberal orientation than their male counterparts. In 2004, 33 percent of men and 38 percent of women indicated that they had a liberal or far left political orientation.

Black students' increased conservatism is reflected in their stances on several political issues. Between 1981 and 2001, student support of abortion rights declined. Whereas six of ten Black undergraduates (59 percent) in 1981 believed abortion should be legal, support for abortion dropped to 53 percent by 2004. Also, while there were decreases between 1981 and 2001, the number of students who thought that laws should prohibit homosexual relationships has increased in 2004. Forty-eight percent of students thought homosexual relationships should be prohibited in 1981, dropping to 28 percent of students who agreed with this statement in 2001, and rising in agreement to 36 percent in 2004.

Interesting trends were also observed with regard to student views on racial issues. There was a very slight increase from 1990 to 2004 in the percentage of Black students who strongly or somewhat agreed with the statement "Racial discrimination is no longer a major problem in America," though students at HBCUs were somewhat more likely to say that racism was irrelevant in 2004 (12 percent in 2004 vs. 10 percent in 1990). Black students were still, however, considerably less likely than 2004 freshmen overall to think that racism had been eradicated (12 vs. 23 percent for all freshmen). The percentage of students who believed affirmative action should be abolished remained consistent in the last decade, with one quarter of students agreeing it should be abolished at both time points. Interestingly, Black students at HBCUs viewed affirmative action less favorably than students at PWIs; 24 percent of PWI and 28 percent of HBCU freshmen felt affirmative action should be abolished in 2004. As expected, Black students tended to view the use of affirmative action policies more positively than their freshman peers. In 2004, 50 percent of incoming freshmen felt affirmative action should be abolished, as compared to 25 percent of Black freshmen.

Students are entering colleges with strong commitments to civic and political participation, coupled with intentions to assume leadership. Students increasingly anticipated involvement in volunteer work during college (19 percent in 1990 vs. 30 percent in 2004). However, students at HBCUs (34 percent) placed higher importance on volunteering compared to students at PWIs (28 percent). While a growing desire was observed among students to influence social values, this increase was more significant for students attending HBCUs (from 39 percent in 1971 to 52 percent in 2004) than those at PWIs (from 41 percent in 1971 to 48 percent in 2004). Black freshmen also placed increased importance on becoming community leaders, with more Black students at HBCUs being committed to community leadership than students at PWIs in 2004 (47 vs. 40 percent). As mentioned above, this trend was accompanied by a large increase in the percentage of students who felt they possessed skills that would help them fulfill these roles.

While there was increased political and civic engagement in some areas, there were decreases elsewhere. In 1971, 41 percent of Black freshmen at PWIs reported that it was "essential" or "very important" to participate in a community action program; by 2004, the proportion of students expressing that this was a personal goal dropped to 31 percent. Students at HBCUs placed greater value on being engaged in community action programs. In 1971, 42 percent considered it very important or essential whereas 38 percent considered this as very important or essential in 2004. Black students at PWIs, however, placed slightly greater emphasis on the need to promote racial understanding than did their counterparts at HBCUs (57 vs. 53 percent in 2004).

SUMMARY, IMPLICATIONS AND CONCLUSIONS

The half-century since the U.S. Supreme Court outlawed Jim Crow segregation has seen significant and dramatic changes regarding the status of Black students in U.S. higher education. The era is best characterized using a "good news-bad news" scenario. Various indicators of status, trends and prospects among African American college students reveal gains, lost ground and a stubbornly persistent status quo of sizeable—often extreme—racial disparities. Debates swirl as to the extent, consequences, causes and solutions of the frequently mentioned Black-White educational achievement gap. In this connection, extensive research summarizes the shifting fortunes of Black college students against a backdrop of sweeping, societal change. As Sedlacek (1999:1) notes: "With issues pertaining to Blacks, people have seen a complex mixture of overt repression, social consciousness, legal changes, backlash, assassinations, political interest, disinterest, and neglect. Higher education has gone about its business during this turbulence." Removal of the blatant barriers of *de jure* racial segregation and disadvantage in college access and success have served to reveal a complex, underlying machinery of *de facto* separate and unequal opportunity structures that perpetuate a status quo where Blacks continue to be significantly underrepresented on the nation's college campuses.

Our report summarizes the status, trends and prospects of African American college freshmen using data collected from 1971 to 2004. Among our key findings:

- The gender gap continues to widen among Black college students. Although it is recognized that Black women enter college at much higher rates than Black men, the proportion of women relative to men has increased steadily since 1971. Moreover, Black women were significantly more likely than men to have "A" averages and the gender gap in achievement at college entry has widened at both PWIs and HBCUs. This trend portends lower college attainment rates for Black males and ultimately, low representation in graduate and professional schools and high status occupations. As it is, Black women were twice as likely to aspire to medical degrees than men—a pattern that is more pronounced among Black students than the general student population.

- Other gender differences were also evident: Black males come from higher socioeconomic backgrounds than their female counterparts and tend to rate themselves more highly on academic ability, intellectual self-confidence, and leadership skills.

- Today, students from the lowest income groups make up a smaller proportion of the total Black freshman population than in 1971. While the percentage has decreased over time, higher concentrations of low-income students can be found at HBCUs compared to PWIs. Conversely, there are more students in the highest income categories than ever before, with parents who are college educated and who work in white-collar professions. However, a significant gap still remains in the parental education levels among Black students relative to the general student population. This pattern is indicative of college admissions and recruitment procedures that privilege more affluent students regardless of color.

- The achievement gap persists between the general population of freshmen and Black students (as indicated by percentage of students who entered college with "A–" or better averages). Despite differences in achievement, their expressed confidence and motivation remained high. In fact, Black students rated themselves higher on intellectual self-confidence and drive to achieve and were more likely to aspire to doctoral degrees than the general student population.

- Black students are now better prepared academically as they enter college. There were declines in the proportion of Black students who stated they required tutoring or remedial education and there were substantial gains between 1984 and 2004 in the proportion who met or exceeded the minimum standard for years of study in English, math, and foreign language as set by the National Commission on Excellence in Education (1983). Black students are now closer to parity with the general freshman population in terms of the number of years in particular content areas. However, more study is needed regarding whether Black students have access to college preparatory courses and quality schools that offer advanced courses: They were somewhat less likely to have met or exceeded the two-year minimum for college-bound students in foreign language and substantially less likely to have done so in physical science.

- There is a mismatch between stated interests and representation of Black students in the sciences. Whereas interest in the sciences has increased over time, and is as high as the general population of freshmen, Black students on today's college campuses continue to be severely underrepresented in the sciences (Pearson & Bechtel, 1989).

- The 2004 data revealed increased interest among Black students in pursuing doctoral degrees. Consistent with the research literature (Allen, 1992), a greater percentage of Black students aspired to doctorates than students in the general freshman population. While their educational aspirations were comparable, Black women were more likely than Black men to view college as preparation for graduate school.

- Black students have become more "middle of the road" and conservative in their political views, as reflected in decreased support for affirmative action, homosexual relationships, and abortion rights. However, they continue to be more liberal than the general student population.

- Over the past decade, increased numbers of Black students entered college with strong interests in civic and political engagement (e.g., volunteer work, community leadership). This is a particularly significant characteristic of students at HBCUs, where there has been a long tradition of service to communities in need.

Our research findings are illustrative. While college experiences and environments have been found to impact student outcomes significantly (Gurin et al., 2004), Nie and Hillygus (2001) highlight the importance of also understanding students' pre-college qualities and characteristics. Findings from this report hold many implications for evaluating the progress as well as the continuing racial disparities across the higher education landscape. Results highlight the continuing importance of HBCUs in the education of Black students and the production of Black baccalaureates for the nation. At the same time, the role of PWIs has increased in importance over the decades in educating Black students. As we move ahead to meet Justice O'Connor's charge of increasing the pathways to leadership to students of all ethnic and racial identities (*Grutter v. Bollinger*, No. 2-241, Supreme Court, June 23, 2003, 3–4), it is encouraging to note the high levels of interest in college among Black students. However, it is important to continue to explore whether postsecondary institutions are increasing access or mitigating such opportunities.

In *Bakke v. Regents of the University of California* (1978), the U.S. Supreme Court approved affirmative action programs that used race as one factor in college admissions. This decision affirmed the value of diversity in higher education and the correlate need for diversity among the country's leading elite. The decision also recognized the necessity for extraordinary affirmative actions to ensure that established admissions procedures at America's most prestigious universities did not continue to exclude Blacks systematically. Otherwise, the extreme Black-White educational disparity, rooted in historical and contemporary racial inequities, could never be overcome. The debate over affirmative action, however, is not settled. It has raged from *Bakke* to *Grutter*, when the Court again affirmed the importance, value, legality and ultimate fairness of such programs.

The recent Supreme Court decision in the University of Michigan affirmative action case *Grutter v. Bollinger* (2003) emphasizes the critical importance of college education as a qualification for upward mobility in contemporary society (Stohr, 2004). Justice O'Connor specifically notes the importance of equitable access to college opportunities in a diverse democracy:

"Diversity promotes learning outcomes and better prepares students for an increasingly diverse workforce, for society, and for the legal profession. Major American businesses have made clear that the skills needed in today's increasingly global marketplace can only be developed through exposure to widely diverse people, cultures, ideas, and viewpoints. High-ranking retired officers and civilian military leaders assert that a highly qualified, racially diverse officer corps is essential to national security. Moreover, because universities, and in particular, law schools, represent the training ground for a large number of the Nation's leaders . . . the path to leadership must be visibly open to talented and qualified individuals of every race and ethnicity" (Sandra Day O'Connor, writing for the majority in *Grutter v. Bollinger*, No. 2-241, Supreme Court, June 23, 2003, 3–4).

Where equal educational opportunities are not broadly available to people of diverse gender, race, ethnic, social class and regional backgrounds, society's very legitimacy is threatened. The goals of "liberty, justice and the pursuit of happiness" for all still elude our grasp in America. It is to the nation's credit that we as a people continue to renew and insist on the pursuit of these lofty goals; likewise, it is to our shame and failure that significant educational disparities persist from kindergarten to college. Herein lies a major test of this country's aspirations and claims to greatness.

References

Allen, W.R. (1992). The color of success: African American student outcomes at Predominantly White and Historically Black public colleges and universities. *Harvard Educational Review, 62*(1), 26–44.

Antonio, A.L. (2004). The influence of friendship groups on intellectual self-confidence and educational aspirations in college. *Journal of Higher Education, 75,* 446–471.

Astin, A.W. (1982). *Minorities in Higher Education.* San Francisco: Jossey-Bass.

Astin, A. (1990). *The Black Undergraduate: Current Status and Trends in the Characteristics of Freshmen.* Los Angeles, CA: Higher Education Research Institute, Graduate School of Education, University of California, Los Angeles.

Astin, A., Oseguera, L., Sax, L., & Korn, W. (2002). *The American Freshman: Thirty-Five Year Trends.* Los Angeles, CA: Cooperative Institutional Research Program and American Council on Education.

Bakke v. Regents of the University of California, 438 U.S. 265 (1978).

Bowen, W.G., & Bok, D. (1998). *The Shape of the River: Long-Term Consequences of Considering Race in College and University Admissions.* Princeton, NJ: Princeton University Press.

Brown v. Board of Education of Topeka, 347 U.S. 483 (1954).

Brown, M.K., Carnoy, M., Currie, E., Duster, T., Oppenheimer, D.B., Shultz, M.M., & Wellman, D. (2003). *Whitewashing Race: The Myth of a Color-Blind Society.* Berkeley, CA: University of California Press.

Chang, M.J., Astin, A.W., & Kim, D. (2004). Cross-racial interaction among undergraduates: Some consequences, causes, and patterns. *Research in Higher Education, 45*, 529–553.

Chang, M.J., Denson, N., Saenz, V., & Misa, K. (in press). The educational benefits of sustaining cross-racial interaction among undergraduates. *Journal of Higher Education*.

Chang, M.J., Witt, D., Jones, J., & Hakuta, K. (2003). *Compelling Interest: Examining the Evidence on Racial Dynamics in Colleges and Universities.* Stanford, CA: Stanford University Press.

Executive Order No. 11246, 3 C.F.R., 1965 Supp., p. 167 (1965).

Fleming, J. (1984). *Blacks in College.* San Francisco: Jossey-Bass.

Grutter v. Bollinger, 539 U.S. 306 (2003).

Gurin, P., Dey, E.L., Hurtado, S., & Gurin, G. (2002). Diversity in higher education: Theory and impact on educational outcomes. *Harvard Educational Review, 72*(3), 330–366.

Gurin, P., Lehman, J.S., Hurtado, S., Lewis, E., Dey, E.L., & Gurin, G. (2004). *Defending Diversity: Affirmative Action at the University of Michigan.* Ann Arbor, MI: University of Michigan Press.

Harvey, W.B., & Anderson, E.L. (2005). *Minorities in Higher Education: Twenty-First Annual Status Report.* Washington, DC: American Council on Education.

Holland, D. (1990). *Educated in Romance: Women, Achievement, and College Culture.* Chicago, IL: University of Chicago Press.

Hurtado, S. (1992). The campus racial climate: Contexts of conflict. *Journal of Higher Education, 63*, 539–569.

Johnson, L.B. (1965, June 4). *To Fulfill These Rights.* Commencement address at Howard University, Washington, DC.

Kozol, J. (2005). *Shame of a Nation.* New York: Crown Publishers.

McDonough, P. (1998). Structuring college opportunities: A cross-case analysis of organizational cultures, climates, and habiti. In C. Torres & T. Mitchell (Eds.), *Sociology of Education: Emerging Perspectives* (pp. 181–210). New York: SUNY Press.

McDonough, P.M., Antonio, A.L., & Trent, J.W. (1997). Black students, Black colleges: An African American college choice model. *Journal for a Just and Caring Education, 3*, 9–36.

Morris, A.D. (1984). *The Origins of the Civil Rights Movement: Black Communities Organizing for Change*. New York: Free Press.

National Commission on Excellence in Education (1983). *A Nation at Risk: The Imperative for Educational Reform*. Washington, DC: U.S. Government Printing Office.

Nie, N., & Hillygus, D.S. (2001). Education and democratic citizenship. In C.L. Glenn, G. Grant, D.S. Hillygus, M. Holmes, N.H. Nie, W.A. Nord, R.D. Putnam, J.N. Rakove, D. Ravitch, R.C. Salomone, J.P. Viteritti, & A. Wolfe (Eds.), *Education and Civil Society* (pp. 30–59). New York: Yale University Press.

Oakes, J., Mendoza, J., & Silver, D. (2004). *California Opportunity Indicators: Informing and Monitoring California's Progress Toward Equitable College Access*. Los Angeles, CA: University of California All Campus Consortium on Research for Diversity (UC/ACCORD).

Omi, M., & Winant, H. (1994). *Racial Formation in the United States: From the 1960s to the 1990s*. New York: Routledge.

Pearson, W. Jr., & Bechtel, H.K. (Eds.) (1989). *Blacks, Science, and American Education*. New Brunswick, NJ: Rutgers University Press.

Pincus, F.L. (2003). *Reverse Discrimination: Dismantling the Myth*. Boulder, CO: Lynne Rienner.

Plessy v. Ferguson, 163 U.S. 537 (1896).

Sax, L.J., Hurtado, S., Lindholm, J.A., Astin, A.W., Korn, W.S., & Mahoney, K.M. (2004). *The American Freshman: National Norms*. Los Angeles, CA: Higher Education Research Institute and American Council on Education.

Sedlacek, W. (1999). Black students on white campuses: 20 years of research. *Journal of College Student Development*, Sept/October, 538–550.

Stanton-Salazar, R. (2001). *Manufacturing Hope and Despair: The School and Kin Support Networks of U.S.-Mexican Youth*. Sociology of Education Series, No. 9. New York: Teachers College Press.

Stohr, G. (2004). *A Black and White Case: How Affirmative Action Survived Its Greatest Legal Challenge*. Princeton, NJ: Bloomberg Press.

United States Kerner Commission. (1968). *Report of the National Advisory Commission on Civil Disorders*. With an Introduction by T. Wicker. New York: Bantam Books.

Appendix

The 1971 and 2004 National Norms for Black Students by Gender and Type of Institutions

ITEM	1971 ALL·ALL	1971 ALL·PWI	1971 ALL·HBCU	1971 MEN·ALL	1971 MEN·PWI	1971 MEN·HBCU	1971 WOMEN·ALL	1971 WOMEN·PWI	1971 WOMEN·HBCU	2004 ALL·ALL	2004 ALL·PWI	2004 ALL·HBCU	2004 MEN·ALL	2004 MEN·PWI	2004 MEN·HBCU	2004 WOMEN·ALL	2004 WOMEN·PWI	2004 WOMEN·HBCU
Number of Respondents	11,743	5,080	5,080	5,304	2,463	2,463	6,439	2,617	2,617	21,537	16,798	16,798	8,174	6,576	6,576	13,363	10,222	10,222
Citizenship status [1972]																		
Yes	97.3	95.6	99.4	97.7	96.5	99.3	96.9	94.9	99.5	96.3	95.2	98.4	96.1	94.6	98.6	96.5	95.6	98.2
No	2.7	4.4	0.6	2.3	3.5	0.7	3.1	5.1	0.5	3.7	4.8	1.6	3.9	5.4	1.4	3.5	4.4	1.8
Your religious preference [1973]																		
Baptist	50.9	45.4	57.6	51.7	46.0	58.2	50.2	44.9	57.0	44.0	38.8	52.6	44.2	39.2	52.5	43.8	38.6	52.7
Buddhist	—	—	—	—	—	—	—	—	—	0.2	0.3	0.1	0.2	0.2	0.1	0.2	0.3	0.1
Congregational (UCC)	0.8	0.6	0.9	0.6	0.5	0.7	0.9	0.7	1.1	0.7	0.6	0.9	0.6	0.5	0.1	0.8	0.6	1.0
Eastern Orthodox	0.0	0.0	0.0	0.0	0.0	0.0	0.0	0.0	0.0	0.4	0.6	0.0	0.6	0.9	0.1	0.2	0.4	0.0
Episcopal	2.5	2.9	2.0	2.5	2.5	1.3	2.9	3.2	2.6	1.4	1.4	1.3	1.3	1.5	1.0	1.4	1.3	1.6
Jewish	0.2	0.3	0.0	0.3	0.3	0.0	0.2	0.2	0.1	0.2	0.3	0.0	0.3	0.4	0.1	0.1	0.2	0.0
Latter Day Saints (Mormon)	0.0	0.0	0.0	0.0	0.0	0.0	0.0	0.0	0.0	0.1	0.2	0.0	0.1	0.1	0.1	0.2	0.2	0.1
Lutheran	1.6	2.2	0.8	2.3	2.3	0.6	1.6	2.2	0.9	1.0	1.3	0.6	0.9	1.1	0.6	1.1	1.3	0.6
Methodist	14.7	12.3	17.5	12.0	12.0	16.3	15.2	12.5	18.7	5.2	4.5	6.3	4.9	4.4	5.9	5.4	4.6	6.7
Muslim (Islamic)	0.4	0.5	0.3	0.8	0.8	0.5	0.3	0.3	0.2	1.1	1.2	1.1	1.1	1.1	1.1	1.2	1.3	1.0
Presbyterian	2.5	2.5	2.6	1.8	1.8	2.6	2.8	3.0	2.6	1.2	1.4	1.0	1.3	1.5	1.1	1.2	1.3	0.9
Quaker (Society of Friends)	0.1	0.1	0.1	0.2	0.2	0.0	0.1	0.1	0.1	0.1	0.1	0.0	0.1	0.1	0.1	0.1	0.1	0.0
Roman Catholic	10.4	12.6	7.8	12.4	12.4	8.3	10.4	12.7	7.5	7.2	8.4	5.2	7.2	8.3	5.4	7.2	8.4	5.0
Seventh Day Adventist	0.6	1.0	0.2	0.7	0.7	0.2	0.8	1.2	0.2	1.2	1.1	1.2	1.0	1.0	0.8	1.3	1.2	1.5
Unitarian Universalist	0.1	0.2	0.1	0.2	0.2	0.0	0.1	0.1	0.1	0.1	0.1	0.1	0.1	0.2	0.0	0.1	0.1	0.1
Other Christian (Protestant)	3.1	4.1	2.0	3.7	3.7	2.1	3.3	4.4	1.8	22.0	23.7	19.3	21.7	22.9	19.7	22.2	24.1	19.0
Other religion	4.5	5.1	3.6	4.6	4.6	3.4	4.8	5.5	3.9	4.3	4.4	4.2	3.6	3.8	3.3	4.8	4.8	4.7
None	7.5	10.2	4.4	11.9	11.9	5.5	6.5	8.9	3.4	9.6	11.8	6.0	10.9	12.8	7.7	8.8	11.0	4.9
What is the best estimate of your parents' total income last year? Consider income from all sources before taxes.																		
Less than $6,000	41.0	38.8	43.2	38.6	35.1	42.2	43.1	42.0	44.2	—	—	—	—	—	—	—	—	—
$6,000 to $9,999 (Less than $10,000 in 2004)	28.5	30.0	27.1	28.3	29.8	26.8	28.7	30.1	27.3	10.2	9.2	12.0	8.9	7.6	11.1	11.1	10.2	12.6
$10,000 to $14,999	18.1	19.6	16.6	19.9	22.1	17.6	16.7	17.4	15.9	6.3	5.9	7.1	5.7	5.4	6.2	6.8	6.2	7.7
$15,000 to $19,999	6.1	6.1	6.1	6.8	7.0	6.6	5.5	5.4	5.6	5.8	5.6	6.1	4.9	4.8	5.1	6.4	6.2	6.8
$20,000 to $24,999	3.1	3.0	3.2	3.1	3.1	3.2	3.1	2.9	3.3	7.8	7.5	8.4	7.1	6.3	8.4	8.3	8.3	6.8
$25,000 to $29,999	1.3	1.1	1.5	1.2	1.2	1.5	1.3	1.0	1.5	6.8	6.9	6.5	6.6	6.4	6.8	6.9	7.3	6.3
$30,000 to $39,999	—	—	—	—	—	—	—	—	—	10.8	11.2	10.3	10.5	10.9	9.8	11.1	11.3	10.6
$30,000 to $34,999	0.7	0.6	0.9	0.5	0.5	0.7	0.8	0.6	1.0	—	—	—	—	—	—	—	—	—
$35,000 to $39,999	0.3	0.2	0.4	0.4	0.4	0.4	0.3	0.1	0.5	—	—	—	—	—	—	—	—	—
$40,000 or more	0.7	0.6	0.9	0.7	0.7	1.1	0.6	0.5	0.8	—	—	—	—	—	—	—	—	—
$40,000 to $49,999	—	—	—	—	—	—	—	—	—	9.8	9.7	10.0	9.6	9.4	9.9	10.0	10.0	10.1
$50,000 to $59,999	—	—	—	—	—	—	—	—	—	9.1	9.1	9.1	9.4	9.3	9.6	8.8	8.9	8.6
$60,000 to $74,999	—	—	—	—	—	—	—	—	—	10.1	10.5	9.4	10.6	11.2	9.6	9.8	10.1	9.3
$75,000 to $99,999	—	—	—	—	—	—	—	—	—	9.8	10.1	9.4	10.8	11.6	9.5	9.1	9.0	9.3
$100,000 to $149,999	—	—	—	—	—	—	—	—	—	7.9	8.4	7.2	9.1	9.6	8.4	7.1	7.6	6.3
$150,000 to $199,999	—	—	—	—	—	—	—	—	—	2.8	2.9	2.5	3.6	3.9	3.2	2.2	2.3	2.0
$200,000 or more	—	—	—	—	—	—	—	—	—	2.6	3.0	2.1	3.1	3.6	2.3	2.3	2.5	2.0
What is the highest level of formal education obtained by your father?																		
Grammar school or less	20.4	19.6	21.3	19.5	19.5	20.8	20.6	19.7	21.6	3.4	3.1	3.9	3.3	3.3	3.4	3.5	3.0	4.2
Some high school	28.3	28.0	28.7	28.0	26.5	29.6	28.6	29.3	27.9	8.5	8.2	9.0	7.5	7.3	7.9	9.2	8.8	9.8
High school graduate	26.6	27.8	25.3	26.9	28.0	25.8	26.3	27.7	24.9	30.6	29.0	33.2	29.7	27.7	33.1	31.1	29.9	33.3
Postsecondary school other than college	—	—	—	—	—	—	—	—	—	4.4	4.4	4.4	4.2	4.4	4.0	4.4	4.3	4.6
Some college	11.1	12.0	10.1	11.9	11.9	9.6	11.3	12.1	10.5	19.3	19.3	19.2	18.1	18.0	18.3	20.1	20.3	19.8
College degree	8.4	8.0	8.9	9.3	9.3	8.8	7.9	6.8	9.0	19.7	20.4	18.6	21.4	22.4	19.9	18.6	19.1	17.6
Some graduate school	—	—	—	—	—	—	—	—	—	1.3	1.4	1.0	1.5	1.5	1.5	1.2	1.4	0.7
Graduate degree	5.2	4.6	5.8	4.9	4.9	5.4	5.3	4.4	6.1	12.9	14.1	10.8	14.2	15.6	12.0	11.9	13.1	9.9

NOTE: Results in italics were taken from year(s) other than 1971 or 2004, because the questions on which the results are based were not asked in those year(s). The actual year from which the results were taken is indicated in Item column.

What is the highest level of formal education obtained by your mother?

ITEM	1971 ALL			1971 MEN			1971 WOMEN			2004 ALL			2004 MEN			2004 WOMEN		
	ALL	PWI	HBCU	ALL	PWI	HBCU	ALL	PWI	HBCU	ALL	PWI	HBCU	ALL	PWI	HBCU	ALL	PWI	HBCU
Grammar school or less	9.4	9.0	9.8	9.6	9.5	9.8	9.2	8.6	9.8	2.7	2.8	2.4	2.7	3.1	2.0	2.7	2.7	2.6
Some high school	28.5	28.4	28.5	28.5	27.4	29.6	28.5	29.3	27.7	5.9	6.2	5.3	5.3	5.7	4.6	6.3	6.5	5.9
High school graduate	33.0	34.9	31.0	33.7	35.7	31.6	32.4	34.2	30.5	22.2	21.4	23.7	22.1	21.3	23.4	22.4	21.4	23.9
Postsecondary school other than college	—	—	—	—	—	—	—	—	—	5.1	5.5	4.4	4.7	5.2	3.8	5.4	5.7	4.8
Some college	13.9	15.0	12.7	12.6	13.9	11.2	14.9	15.9	14.0	23.7	23.3	24.3	22.3	21.2	24.1	24.6	24.8	24.4
College degree	10.5	8.9	12.2	11.0	9.8	12.1	10.2	8.2	12.2	24.7	24.7	24.8	26.4	26.4	26.3	23.6	23.5	23.8
Some graduate school	—	—	—	—	—	—	—	—	—	2.2	2.4	1.9	2.0	2.2	1.6	2.3	2.5	2.1
Graduate degree	4.8	3.7	5.8	4.6	3.6	5.7	4.9	3.9	5.9	13.5	13.8	13.1	14.7	15.0	14.2	12.8	13.0	12.4
Your father's occupation																		
Artist	0.7	0.8	0.7	0.7	0.9	0.5	0.8	0.7	0.8	1.0	1.1	0.8	1.3	1.5	1.1	0.8	0.8	0.6
Business	7.5	7.5	7.4	7.7	8.2	7.2	7.2	6.8	7.7	15.6	16.3	14.6	17.4	18.4	15.7	14.5	14.9	13.9
Clerical	1.2	1.6	0.8	1.4	2.0	0.9	1.1	1.4	0.8	1.7	1.6	1.9	1.6	1.3	2.0	0.9	1.1	1.0
Clergy	1.8	1.6	2.0	1.6	1.1	2.0	2.0	2.0	2.0	0.6	0.8	1.6	0.7	0.9	1.5	0.5	0.7	1.9
College teacher	0.7	0.6	0.7	0.7	0.7	0.7	0.6	0.5	0.7	1.3	1.6	0.8	1.5	2.0	0.6	1.2	1.3	0.3
Doctor (MD or DDS)	0.9	0.7	1.0	0.8	0.8	0.8	1.0	0.7	1.2	2.4	2.5	2.1	2.6	2.7	2.4	2.2	2.4	0.9
Education (secondary)	3.3	2.6	4.0	3.3	2.5	4.2	3.3	2.6	3.9	0.9	0.8	2.1	1.0	0.9	2.4	0.8	0.8	2.0
Education (elementary)	0.7	0.5	0.9	0.7	0.5	1.0	0.7	0.6	0.8	0.9	0.8	0.9	1.0	0.9	1.1	0.8	0.8	0.8
Engineer	2.4	2.4	2.3	2.9	2.1	2.7	2.7	2.8	2.0	6.1	6.3	5.8	6.9	6.6	7.5	5.6	6.1	4.7
Farmer or forester	4.3	2.8	5.7	4.4	2.9	6.0	4.2	2.8	5.5	0.4	0.4	0.5	0.5	0.6	0.3	0.4	0.3	0.6
Health professional	1.2	1.1	1.2	1.2	1.2	1.3	1.1	1.0	1.2	1.3	1.4	1.2	1.5	1.5	1.5	1.2	1.3	1.0
Homemaker	0.3	0.1	0.2	0.2	0.1	0.4	0.2	0.4	0.2	0.2	0.2	0.1	0.2	0.3	0.2	0.2	0.2	0.1
Lawyer	0.3	0.4	0.3	0.2	0.3	0.4	0.3	0.4	0.2	1.0	1.1	0.8	1.3	1.4	1.0	0.9	1.0	0.7
Military	2.8	2.7	2.9	3.0	3.5	2.6	2.6	2.1	3.1	4.4	4.1	5.0	4.3	4.2	4.6	4.5	4.0	5.2
Nurse	0.2	0.1	0.3	0.2	0.2	0.3	0.2	0.1	0.4	0.8	0.9	0.8	0.9	1.1	0.7	0.8	0.8	0.8
Research scientist	0.3	0.4	0.3	0.3	0.3	0.3	0.2	0.4	0.1	0.2	0.3	0.1	0.2	0.3	0.1	0.2	0.2	0.2
Social worker	0.7	0.7	0.7	0.6	0.6	0.8	0.7	0.8	0.6	1.1	1.2	1.0	1.5	1.5	1.4	0.9	1.0	0.8
Skilled worker	13.2	13.6	12.9	13.7	13.0	14.5	12.9	14.0	11.7	7.6	7.4	8.0	8.5	8.3	8.9	7.1	6.8	7.5
Semi skilled worker	16.4	17.5	15.2	18.8	20.5	17.0	14.5	15.1	13.9	3.8	3.7	4.1	3.8	3.7	3.9	3.9	3.7	4.2
Laborer	14.8	16.5	12.9	15.1	16.8	13.2	14.5	16.3	12.7	3.9	4.0	3.9	3.9	3.8	4.0	4.0	4.1	3.8
Unemployed	4.1	4.2	3.9	3.1	2.8	3.5	4.8	5.3	4.3	7.0	6.7	7.4	5.3	5.0	5.7	8.1	7.8	8.5
Other occupation	22.5	21.5	23.4	19.6	19.0	20.1	24.8	23.6	25.9	37.3	36.6	38.6	33.7	32.7	35.4	39.8	39.3	40.6
Your mother's occupation																		
Artist	0.3	0.2	0.4	0.3	0.2	0.4	0.3	0.3	0.4	0.8	0.9	0.5	0.8	1.1	0.3	0.7	0.8	0.6
Business	2.6	2.8	2.4	2.2	2.1	2.3	3.0	3.4	2.5	16.5	16.2	17.1	17.6	17.3	18.2	15.8	15.5	16.4
Clerical	4.5	5.4	3.6	4.0	5.2	2.8	4.9	5.5	4.3	5.0	5.2	4.7	4.8	5.3	4.0	5.2	5.2	5.2
Clergy	0.1	0.1	0.1	0.1	0.1	0.1	0.0	0.0	0.1	0.4	0.4	0.3	0.4	0.5	0.3	0.4	0.3	0.3
College teacher	0.4	0.3	0.6	0.4	0.2	0.7	0.5	0.5	0.5	0.4	0.4	0.3	0.4	0.5	0.3	0.4	0.3	0.7
Doctor (MD or DDS)	0.1	0.1	0.2	0.1	0.1	0.1	0.2	0.1	0.2	0.8	0.9	0.7	0.8	0.9	0.7	0.8	0.8	0.7
Education (secondary)	3.5	3.0	4.1	3.8	3.4	4.2	3.4	2.7	4.1	4.3	4.1	4.8	4.7	4.4	5.0	4.1	3.8	4.7
Education (elementary)	7.4	5.5	9.3	7.5	6.1	9.1	7.2	5.0	9.4	6.6	6.3	7.1	7.0	6.6	7.6	6.4	6.1	6.8
Engineer	0.1	0.0	0.1	0.1	0.1	0.1	0.0	0.0	0.1	0.8	0.6	1.1	0.8	0.7	1.2	0.7	0.5	1.0
Farmer or forester	0.1	0.0	0.2	0.1	0.1	0.2	0.1	0.0	0.1	0.1	0.2	0.1	0.2	0.2	0.2	0.1	0.1	0.0
Health professional	1.5	1.2	1.9	1.3	1.2	1.4	1.8	1.3	2.3	2.6	2.6	2.5	2.4	2.4	2.5	2.7	2.8	2.6
Homemaker	35.2	37.9	32.5	36.6	39.7	33.3	34.1	36.4	31.8	3.4	4.0	2.3	2.7	3.5	1.4	3.8	4.3	2.9
Lawyer	0.0	0.0	0.0	0.0	0.0	0.1	0.0	0.0	0.0	0.7	0.7	0.7	0.7	0.7	0.7	0.7	0.6	0.7
Military	0.0	0.0	0.1	0.0	0.0	0.1	0.0	0.0	0.0	0.8	0.8	0.9	0.9	0.9	0.7	0.8	0.7	1.0
Nurse	6.7	7.4	6.0	6.3	6.2	6.5	7.0	8.4	5.6	10.7	11.0	10.2	11.6	12.0	11.0	10.1	10.3	9.8
Research scientist	0.1	0.1	0.0	0.1	0.1	0.0	0.1	0.1	0.1	0.1	0.2	0.0	0.2	0.2	0.1	0.1	0.1	0.0
Social worker	1.9	1.7	2.2	1.7	2.0	2.4	1.8	1.5	2.0	3.5	3.6	3.5	3.9	3.8	4.0	3.3	3.4	3.1
Skilled worker	2.8	2.6	3.0	2.5	2.3	2.8	3.0	2.9	3.1	1.8	1.9	1.7	2.3	2.5	1.9	1.6	1.5	1.6
Semi skilled worker	6.7	6.5	7.0	7.0	6.4	7.6	6.6	6.5	6.6	2.1	2.2	2.0	2.3	2.4	2.2	2.0	2.1	1.8
Laborer	4.8	4.4	5.1	5.0	4.7	5.3	4.6	4.2	5.0	2.0	2.1	1.8	2.0	2.1	1.7	2.0	2.1	1.9
Unemployed	5.5	6.0	5.0	6.0	6.5	5.5	5.1	5.7	4.5	6.8	6.7	6.9	6.0	5.9	6.2	7.3	7.2	7.3
Other occupation	15.5	14.6	16.4	14.4	13.6	15.2	16.4	15.5	17.3	29.8	29.2	30.8	27.5	26.0	30.0	31.3	31.3	31.3

ITEM	1971									2004								
	ALL			MEN			WOMEN			ALL			MEN			WOMEN		
	ALL	PWI	HBCU	ALL	PWI	HBCU	ALL	PWI	HBCU	ALL	PWI	HBCU	ALL	PWI	HBCU	ALL	PWI	HBCU
Do you have any concern about your ability to finance your college education?																		
None (I am confident that I will have sufficient funds)	18.2	16.7	19.8	21.7	21.3	22.2	15.4	12.9	17.9	26.4	24.3	29.9	33.3	31.7	36.0	21.7	19.3	25.8
Some (but I probably will have enough funds)	55.7	56.3	55.1	55.0	55.4	54.6	56.3	57.0	55.6	50.8	52.5	47.8	48.4	49.8	46.0	52.4	54.3	49.1
Major (not sure I will have enough funds)	26.0	27.0	25.0	23.3	23.3	23.3	28.3	30.1	26.5	22.9	23.2	22.3	18.3	18.5	18.1	25.9	26.4	25.1
Received $1,500 or more of my educational expenses (room, board, tuition, and fees) from: *[1981, 2000]*																		
Parents, other relatives or friends	15.4	16.6	13.5	15.4	16.8	13.5	15.3	16.4	13.6	41.9	42.5	40.9	42.4	42.8	41.9	41.5	42.4	40.2
Spouse	0.2	0.3	0.2	0.5	0.6	0.3	0.0	0.0	0.1	0.2	0.3	0.3	0.4	0.5	0.3	0.1	0.1	0.3
Savings from summer work	0.8	0.9	0.5	1.2	1.6	0.7	0.4	0.5	0.4	3.1	3.8	2.1	3.8	4.6	2.6	2.6	3.2	1.8
Other savings	0.6	0.5	0.7	0.5	0.4	0.7	0.6	0.5	0.8	3.9	3.9	3.7	4.1	4.2	4.1	3.7	3.8	3.4
Part time job on campus	—	—	—	—	—	—	—	—	—	4.0	5.5	1.7	3.7	5.3	1.4	4.2	5.6	1.9
Part time job off campus	0.7	0.8	0.5	0.9	1.1	0.5	0.5	0.6	0.5	2.4	3.1	1.4	2.6	3.2	1.7	2.3	3.0	1.2
Full time job while in college	0.5	0.4	0.5	0.6	0.7	0.6	0.3	0.2	0.4	1.6	1.7	1.3	1.9	1.9	1.9	1.4	1.6	1.0
Pell Grant	17.1	16.9	17.5	16.7	16.0	17.8	17.5	17.6	17.3	21.3	19.7	23.6	18.5	17.7	19.5	23.2	21.0	26.6
Supplemental Educational Opportunity Grant (SEOG)	2.0	2.0	2.1	2.4	2.0	2.2	2.0	1.9	2.0	4.9	5.5	3.9	4.7	5.3	3.8	5.0	5.6	4.0
State scholarship or grant	3.4	4.0	2.4	3.9	4.6	3.1	3.0	3.7	1.8	13.1	14.7	10.8	11.7	13.1	9.8	14.1	15.7	11.5
College Work-Study Grant	1.2	0.9	1.6	1.3	1.0	2.0	1.1	0.9	1.3	6.5	8.7	3.4	5.3	7.6	2.0	7.4	9.4	4.3
College grant/scholarship (other than above)	4.6	5.6	3.0	4.7	5.6	3.4	4.4	5.6	2.6	23.0	24.1	21.3	21.9	23.8	19.2	23.8	24.4	22.8
Vocational Rehabilitation funds	—	—	—	—	—	—	—	—	—	0.6	0.7	0.5	0.7	0.9	0.5	0.5	0.5	0.5
Other private grant	1.2	1.4	0.9	1.4	1.7	1.1	1.0	1.2	0.7	5.2	5.9	4.3	5.1	5.8	4.2	5.3	6.0	4.3
Other government aid (ROTC, BIA, GI/ military benefits, etc.)	1.7	1.7	1.8	1.7	1.6	1.8	1.8	1.8	1.8	2.6	2.6	2.6	3.2	3.5	2.7	2.3	2.1	2.6
Stafford Loan (GSL)	10.4	11.8	8.2	10.9	13.3	7.5	10.0	10.8	8.7	23.9	20.1	29.5	21.1	18.8	24.4	25.7	21.0	33.1
Perkins Loan (NDSL)	2.6	2.8	2.2	2.4	2.9	1.6	2.7	2.8	2.7	5.9	7.2	3.9	4.9	6.1	3.2	6.6	7.9	4.5
Other college loan	1.1	1.3	0.9	1.2	1.4	0.8	1.1	1.2	0.9	8.7	7.8	10.0	8.2	7.6	9.0	9.0	8.0	10.6
Other loan	1.9	2.0	1.7	1.8	2.0	1.7	1.9	2.0	1.7	7.2	6.0	9.1	6.6	6.0	7.5	7.7	6.0	10.2
Other than above	1.1	1.5	0.6	1.6	2.3	0.5	0.8	0.9	0.6	3.9	3.7	4.1	3.9	4.2	3.5	3.9	3.4	4.6
What was your average grade in high school?																		
A or A+	2.2	3.0	1.4	1.7	2.7	0.6	2.6	3.2	2.0	12.2	13.2	10.5	8.2	8.8	7.0	15.0	16.2	12.9
A–	5.5	6.8	4.2	3.7	5.5	1.8	7.1	8.0	6.2	15.5	17.7	11.7	11.6	14.0	7.7	18.2	20.3	14.5
B+	16.2	17.5	14.8	12.3	14.8	9.8	19.3	19.7	19.0	21.4	22.3	19.9	18.4	20.0	15.7	23.5	23.9	22.9
B	25.4	25.9	24.9	21.2	23.4	19.1	28.8	27.9	29.6	23.5	23.7	23.3	24.2	25.5	22.2	23.0	22.4	24.0
B–	17.0	16.7	17.4	18.5	18.5	18.8	15.9	15.5	16.2	13.2	11.9	15.3	16.9	15.1	19.8	10.6	9.7	12.1
C+	19.6	17.1	22.3	24.1	19.3	28.9	16.0	15.2	16.8	9.0	7.1	12.2	12.0	9.8	15.6	6.9	5.2	9.8
C	13.3	12.2	14.3	17.5	15.1	19.9	9.8	9.9	9.7	5.0	3.9	6.9	8.3	6.4	11.6	2.7	2.1	3.7
D	0.8	0.8	0.7	1.0	0.9	1.1	0.5	0.6	0.4	0.2	0.3	0.2	0.4	0.5	0.3	0.1	0.1	0.1
Student rated self above average or highest 10% as compared with the average person of his/her age in:																		
Academic ability	33.4	39.8	26.8	34.5	42.7	26.1	32.5	37.4	27.4	62.1	64.7	57.7	64.2	66.4	60.5	60.6	63.5	55.8
Artistic ability	13.5	14.7	12.2	15.2	16.0	14.4	12.0	13.6	10.4	30.2	31.1	28.6	34.8	34.1	35.9	27.1	29.2	23.6
Drive to achieve	62.6	65.0	60.1	60.9	64.3	57.5	64.0	65.6	62.3	78.9	78.8	79.0	76.5	76.2	77.2	80.5	80.6	80.3
Leadership ability	38.1	42.2	33.8	43.5	48.1	38.8	33.5	37.3	29.6	66.1	66.0	66.4	68.5	68.2	68.9	64.6	64.5	64.7
Mathematical ability	18.5	22.1	14.7	22.8	28.0	17.5	14.8	17.2	12.4	37.1	36.7	37.7	43.0	43.6	42.0	33.0	32.1	34.7
Public speaking ability	22.9	25.5	20.3	24.6	28.0	21.0	21.5	23.4	19.7	38.5	38.5	38.4	40.0	40.0	40.1	37.4	37.4	37.3
Self confidence (intellectual)	38.9	42.6	35.2	44.2	47.7	40.7	34.5	38.3	30.6	69.2	67.3	72.5	75.5	73.9	78.0	65.0	62.8	68.7
Self confidence (social)	37.0	40.1	33.9	40.6	43.0	38.1	34.1	37.7	30.3	62.8	61.2	65.4	67.4	66.4	69.2	59.6	57.7	62.8
Understanding of others	64.2	66.2	62.2	61.2	63.4	59.0	66.7	68.5	64.8	62.5	63.6	60.5	60.7	62.5	57.7	63.7	64.4	62.4
Writing ability	28.0	29.7	26.2	26.5	28.3	24.7	29.2	30.9	27.4	46.7	47.0	46.3	45.0	45.2	44.6	47.9	48.2	47.4

35

ITEM	1971									2004								
	ALL			MEN			WOMEN			ALL			MEN			WOMEN		
	ALL	PWI	HBCU	ALL	PWI	HBCU	ALL	PWI	HBCU	ALL	PWI	HBCU	ALL	PWI	HBCU	ALL	PWI	HBCU
Student met or exceeded recommended years of high school (grades 9–12) study in the following subjects [1984]																		
English (4 years)	93.1	93.9	92.4	92.1	92.8	91.5	93.9	94.6	93.2	96.5	96.9	95.7	96.0	96.5	95.3	96.7	97.2	95.9
Mathematics (3 years)	82.8	85.0	80.8	85.6	87.5	84.0	80.8	83.3	78.5	97.0	97.3	96.5	96.4	96.7	95.8	97.4	97.7	96.9
Foreign language (2 years)	59.9	62.6	57.3	56.7	59.6	54.3	62.1	64.6	59.6	89.4	91.1	86.4	86.2	88.6	81.9	91.6	92.8	89.5
Physical science (2 years)	46.5	46.3	46.7	52.2	53.5	51.1	42.5	41.5	43.4	45.1	48.0	40.3	47.0	50.9	40.7	43.8	46.0	40.0
Biological science (2 years)	34.4	34.3	34.4	35.2	35.8	34.6	33.8	33.3	34.2	38.8	40.5	36.0	38.1	39.6	35.6	39.2	41.0	36.2
History/American govt. (1 year)	98.4	98.3	98.5	98.6	98.3	98.8	98.3	98.3	98.4	97.0	97.2	96.8	96.8	97.1	96.3	97.2	97.2	97.1
Computer science (1/2 year)	43.0	43.8	42.3	48.0	49.1	47.0	39.6	40.3	38.9	62.4	61.7	63.7	67.2	66.9	67.8	59.2	58.2	60.9
Arts and/or music (1 year)	62.6	63.3	61.9	63.2	63.4	63.0	62.1	63.3	61.0	75.0	74.9	75.1	72.4	71.5	73.9	76.7	77.1	75.9
Do you feel you will need any special tutoring or remedial work in: [2003]																		
English	22.0	25.2	18.7	25.3	27.7	22.8	19.3	23.1	15.3	15.8	17.1	13.6	16.6	18.4	13.9	15.3	16.4	13.4
Reading	12.8	15.4	10.1	14.3	17.1	11.6	11.5	14.0	9.0	6.8	7.2	6.1	7.9	8.8	6.5	6.1	6.3	5.8
Mathematics	56.0	54.0	58.1	50.2	48.3	52.2	60.8	58.6	63.1	44.2	44.8	43.1	37.1	35.7	39.4	48.6	50.2	45.6
Social studies	6.6	7.4	5.8	5.0	5.4	4.6	8.0	9.1	6.7	7.7	7.5	8.0	6.6	6.3	7.1	8.4	8.3	8.7
Science	30.4	32.8	27.9	24.7	27.6	21.7	35.1	37.1	33.1	20.7	21.4	19.6	16.3	16.4	16.1	23.5	24.3	21.9
Foreign language	35.6	33.2	38.1	39.6	36.3	43.0	32.3	30.5	34.0	21.0	21.4	20.5	21.2	20.6	22.0	20.9	21.8	19.4
Reasons noted as very important in deciding to go to college																		
My parents wanted me to go	36.3	31.7	41.0	37.1	34.2	40.1	35.7	29.7	41.7	50.3	47.5	55.0	50.4	47.0	56.1	50.2	47.8	54.3
There was nothing better to do	3.8	3.5	4.1	4.3	3.9	4.6	3.3	3.1	3.6	6.9	6.3	8.0	8.8	7.9	10.4	5.6	5.2	6.3
To be able to get a better job	84.5	80.2	89.0	84.3	80.2	88.6	84.7	80.2	89.3	77.0	75.7	79.3	76.2	74.2	79.4	77.6	76.7	79.2
To be able to make more money	64.0	57.5	70.6	67.2	61.1	73.5	61.3	54.5	68.3	81.7	79.6	85.2	82.9	80.2	87.4	80.8	79.2	83.7
To gain a general education and appreciation of ideas	67.8	65.4	70.2	63.1	61.3	65.0	71.6	68.9	74.4	68.5	67.3	70.5	63.3	61.7	66.1	72.0	71.1	73.6
To learn more about things that interest me	72.0	71.8	72.2	69.0	69.2	68.7	74.5	73.9	75.1	78.3	78.2	78.4	74.0	73.3	75.1	81.2	81.5	80.6
To make me a more cultured person	46.6	40.8	52.7	43.0	37.7	48.7	49.5	43.3	55.9	47.3	47.0	47.7	41.1	40.1	42.6	51.5	51.7	51.2
To prepare for graduate or professional school	55.6	53.1	58.2	54.1	52.9	55.3	56.9	53.3	60.5	68.8	66.8	72.3	57.4	55.0	61.4	76.5	74.7	79.7
Wanted to get away from home [1976]	13.0	12.6	13.4	14.8	14.8	14.7	11.5	10.9	12.4	31.5	30.7	32.8	33.3	32.1	35.3	30.3	29.7	31.2
Reasons noted as very important in influencing student's decision to attend this particular college																		
A college rep. recruited me [1975,1997]	11.9	11.9	12.0	11.9	16.4	15.2	8.6	8.2	9.1	9.8	9.2	10.4	11.3	12.7	9.8	8.8	7.1	10.9
A friend suggested attending [1975,1997]	8.2	7.8	8.8	8.2	8.6	9.1	7.8	7.2	8.6	9.3	9.0	9.7	10.6	10.9	10.2	8.5	7.8	9.3
I wanted to live near home [1983]	17.8	18.9	16.4	14.2	15.8	12.4	20.4	21.1	19.5	19.3	20.6	17.1	15.3	16.6	13.2	21.9	23.2	19.7
I was offered financial assistance [1972]	43.3	45.8	40.1	46.1	50.0	41.2	40.9	42.4	39.1	48.0	50.2	44.2	44.6	45.8	42.6	50.2	53.1	45.4
High school guidance counselor advised me [1993]	10.8	12.3	9.4	10.9	12.3	9.6	10.8	12.3	9.2	11.0	11.1	10.9	11.4	11.2	11.6	10.8	11.0	10.4
My relatives wanted me to come here [1973]	10.8	8.8	12.9	9.8	7.5	12.2	11.6	9.8	13.4	13.8	11.9	16.9	14.6	12.1	18.7	13.3	11.8	15.7
My teacher advised me [1973]	9.7	8.8	10.7	10.7	9.0	12.9	8.8	8.8	8.9	7.0	6.7	7.5	7.9	7.4	8.8	6.3	6.2	6.6
Rankings in national magazines [1995]	12.7	16.4	9.4	11.5	15.7	7.8	13.5	16.9	10.4	18.6	16.6	22.1	15.3	15.6	14.9	20.8	17.2	27.0
This college's graduates gain admission to top graduate/professional schools [1983]	36.1	38.2	33.7	33.4	34.1	32.7	38.0	41.1	34.4	36.7	35.7	38.4	28.4	28.3	28.6	42.2	40.6	45.1
This college's graduates get good jobs [1983]	53.3	56.1	50.1	52.3	54.7	49.8	54.1	57.1	50.4	53.6	53.5	53.8	46.4	47.2	45.2	58.4	57.6	59.8
This college has a good reputation for its social activities [1983]	24.5	23.7	25.3	25.0	24.7	25.3	24.1	23.1	25.3	30.3	30.4	30.3	29.1	28.9	29.3	31.2	31.4	30.9
This college has a very good academic reputation [1972]	57.2	60.2	53.2	54.2	59.2	47.9	59.6	61.0	57.8	58.5	59.7	56.4	49.6	51.8	45.8	64.4	65.0	63.5

| | 1971 | | | | | | | | | 2004 | | | | | | | | |
| | ALL | | | MEN | | | WOMEN | | | ALL | | | MEN | | | WOMEN | | |
ITEM	ALL	PWI	HBCU	ALL	PWI	HBCU	ALL	PWI	HBCU	ALL	PWI	HBCU	ALL	PWI	HBCU	ALL	PWI	HBCU
What is the highest academic degree you intend to obtain anywhere? *[1972]*																		
None	2.2	1.7	2.9	2.3	1.7	3.1	2.1	1.7	2.7	1.9	1.7	2.3	2.5	2.0	3.3	1.5	1.5	1.6
Vocational certificate	—	—	—	—	—	—	—	—	—	0.2	0.2	0.2	0.3	0.2	0.4	0.2	0.2	0.1
Associate (A.A.) or equivalent	1.9	2.4	1.1	1.5	1.8	1.1	2.2	3.0	1.1	0.7	0.6	0.9	1.0	0.8	1.3	0.5	0.4	0.7
Bachelor's (B.A.,B.S.,etc.)	28.0	29.5	25.9	27.7	27.2	28.4	28.2	31.3	23.8	17.0	18.1	15.0	21.5	22.8	19.4	14.0	15.0	12.1
Master's degree (M.A.,M.S.,etc.)	37.2	33.4	42.3	34.1	31.7	37.2	39.7	34.7	46.8	35.9	36.3	35.2	38.9	39.5	37.9	33.9	34.2	33.3
Ph.D. or Ed.D.	16.5	16.4	16.5	17.0	17.6	16.2	16.0	15.5	16.8	23.7	22.7	25.3	20.8	20.0	22.2	25.6	24.6	27.3
M.D., D.D.S., D.V.M. or D.O.	7.2	8.9	4.9	7.8	9.6	5.6	6.6	8.3	4.3	12.3	12.0	12.7	7.5	7.3	7.9	15.5	15.2	15.9
LL.B. or J.D. (law)	5.6	6.1	4.9	7.6	8.5	6.5	3.9	4.2	3.6	5.9	6.0	5.8	4.7	5.0	4.1	6.8	6.6	7.0
B.D. or M.Div. (divinity)	0.4	0.3	0.5	0.6	0.5	0.8	0.2	0.2	0.2	0.5	0.4	0.6	0.7	0.5	1.0	0.3	0.3	0.3
Other	1.2	1.3	1.1	1.3	1.3	1.2	1.1	1.3	0.9	1.9	1.9	2.0	2.1	1.9	2.5	1.8	1.8	1.6
Student's Estimates: Chances are very good that he/she will																		
Be satisfied with your college	55.4	53.7	57.3	53.4	50.5	56.5	57.1	56.3	57.9	47.1	48.6	44.5	40.7	43.5	36.2	51.3	52.0	50.1
Change career choice	10.0	10.6	9.2	9.7	11.1	8.3	10.2	10.3	10.1	9.4	10.1	8.3	8.9	9.8	7.5	9.7	10.2	8.8
Change major field	11.6	12.0	11.1	11.2	11.9	10.4	11.9	12.1	11.6	10.9	11.6	9.8	11.3	12.1	10.0	10.7	11.3	9.6
Get a job to help pay for college expenses *[1976]*	26.7	30.2	22.3	26.7	30.1	22.4	26.8	30.2	22.3	47.2	50.7	41.4	38.8	41.6	34.3	52.8	56.6	46.3
Make at least a "B" average	19.5	22.3	16.7	19.6	22.8	16.4	19.4	21.9	16.9	63.2	61.0	66.8	58.8	57.6	60.8	66.1	63.2	70.9
Participate in volunteer or community service work *[1990]*	19.4	19.9	19.0	13.3	13.9	12.6	23.3	23.8	23.0	30.1	28.1	33.5	17.9	16.8	19.6	38.2	35.4	42.9
Seek personal counseling	11.9	11.9	11.9	12.5	13.0	11.9	11.4	11.0	11.9	12.2	12.8	11.1	9.5	9.7	9.1	14.0	14.9	12.4
Transfer to another college before graduating	7.8	8.1	7.4	7.0	7.2	6.7	8.5	8.9	8.1	10.6	9.9	11.7	11.5	10.7	12.8	10.0	9.3	11.0
Work full time while attending college *[1982]*	4.5	5.0	3.7	4.5	5.3	3.6	4.4	4.9	3.8	9.0	9.1	8.8	7.2	6.9	7.7	10.2	10.6	9.6
Objectives considered to be essential or very important																		
Becoming accomplished in one of the performing arts (acting, dancing, etc.)	15.0	13.9	16.2	14.2	13.0	15.4	15.7	14.7	16.9	20.3	19.5	21.5	21.4	19.8	24.0	19.5	19.4	19.8
Becoming a community leader	26.6	26.2	27.2	32.1	32.2	32.0	22.2	21.2	23.2	42.6	40.2	46.5	42.2	39.9	45.9	42.8	40.3	47.0
Becoming an authority in my field	73.4	72.2	74.7	74.8	74.2	75.4	72.3	70.6	74.1	69.5	67.2	73.4	69.7	67.7	72.9	69.5	66.9	73.8
Becoming involved in programs to clean up the environment	38.3	37.3	39.3	40.3	40.0	40.7	36.6	35.0	38.2	24.5	22.3	28.2	25.8	23.0	30.4	23.7	21.9	26.7
Becoming successful in a business of my own	51.0	47.3	55.0	60.4	56.0	65.1	43.4	40.1	46.8	60.1	56.9	65.4	63.6	60.9	68.1	57.7	54.3	63.5
Being very well off financially	53.7	49.5	58.0	60.6	55.4	66.2	48.0	44.7	51.4	87.1	86.1	88.8	85.7	84.7	87.4	88.0	87.0	89.7
Creating artistic work (painting, sculpture, decorating, etc.)	12.9	12.9	12.8	12.2	11.5	13.0	13.4	14.2	12.6	16.3	16.6	15.6	18.1	17.7	18.8	15.0	15.9	13.5
Developing a meaningful philosophy of life	69.9	70.3	69.5	69.7	71.1	68.2	70.1	69.6	70.6	48.7	47.0	51.5	47.6	46.3	49.7	49.4	47.4	52.7
Having administrative responsibility for the work of others	28.7	27.9	29.7	33.6	32.1	35.1	24.8	24.3	25.3	45.6	43.3	49.5	46.8	44.8	50.2	44.8	42.3	48.9
Helping others who are in difficulty	72.9	74.1	71.7	68.9	70.8	66.9	76.2	76.8	75.6	72.8	71.5	75.0	66.3	64.6	69.2	77.2	76.1	79.0
Influencing social values	40.1	41.4	38.8	41.8	44.0	39.5	38.7	39.2	38.1	49.1	47.5	51.9	44.4	42.7	47.2	52.3	50.6	55.1
Influencing the political structure	22.8	23.1	22.5	28.7	28.9	28.4	18.0	18.2	17.7	27.6	25.4	31.3	29.5	27.4	33.0	26.3	24.0	30.1
Keeping up to date with political affairs	44.0	42.6	45.4	49.4	48.7	50.1	39.6	37.6	41.7	37.3	35.6	40.1	38.8	37.4	41.0	36.3	34.5	39.4
Making a theoretical contribution to science	11.6	12.0	11.2	14.8	15.4	14.1	9.0	9.1	8.9	23.2	21.3	26.4	24.3	21.9	28.1	22.5	20.9	25.2
Obtaining recognition from my colleagues for contributions to my special field	51.7	48.4	55.2	56.4	52.9	60.0	47.9	44.7	51.3	59.5	57.4	63.1	60.9	58.3	65.2	58.6	56.8	61.7
Participating in a community action program	41.6	41.4	41.8	41.6	41.8	41.4	41.6	41.1	42.2	33.8	31.2	38.1	29.0	26.2	33.7	36.9	34.5	41.0
Helping to promote racial understanding *[1977]*	70.5	72.0	67.8	69.8	71.5	66.8	71.1	72.4	68.6	55.6	57.4	52.7	51.1	52.4	48.9	58.7	60.7	55.3
Raising a family *[1977]*	53.2	54.0	51.7	57.6	58.4	56.2	49.7	50.6	47.9	72.6	71.3	74.7	74.9	73.6	76.8	71.1	69.7	73.3
Writing original works (poems, novels, short stories, etc.)	14.8	15.6	13.9	14.3	15.5	13.0	15.2	15.7	14.6	21.5	21.5	21.4	21.4	20.9	22.1	21.5	21.9	20.9

37

ITEM	1971 ALL			1971 MEN			1971 WOMEN			2004 ALL			2004 MEN			2004 WOMEN		
	ALL	PWI	HBCU	ALL	PWI	HBCU	ALL	PWI	HBCU	ALL	PWI	HBCU	ALL	PWI	HBCU	ALL	PWI	HBCU
Student agrees strongly or somewhat																		
Abortion should be legal [1977]	58.3	57.6	59.5	55.8	54.7	57.6	60.4	59.9	61.2	52.7	54.0	50.6	51.7	53.3	49.1	53.4	54.4	51.7
Affirmative action in college admissions should be abolished [1995]	25.1	22.4	27.5	28.5	25.8	31.0	22.9	20.2	25.4	25.3	23.7	28.1	28.6	26.9	31.4	23.1	21.5	25.9
College officials have the right to ban persons with extreme views from speaking on campus	23.1	20.7	25.5	24.1	21.8	26.5	22.2	19.7	24.7	43.6	44.1	42.7	46.0	47.4	43.7	42.0	41.9	42.0
It is important to have laws prohibiting homosexual relationships [1981]	47.9	44.8	50.8	57.1	53.2	59.9	43.0	37.6	45.6	36.0	32.6	41.9	45.9	41.5	53.2	29.4	26.6	34.2
Marijuana should be legalized	34.6	36.0	33.2	40.9	41.1	40.7	29.5	31.9	27.0	37.7	36.6	39.4	45.9	45.1	47.2	32.1	30.9	34.2
Racial discrimination is no longer a major problem in America [1990]	10.2	9.5	10.8	12.2	11.2	13.2	8.8	8.3	9.3	12.3	11.5	13.5	15.3	14.8	16.0	10.2	9.3	11.8
Realistically, an individual can do little to bring about change in our society	46.0	45.7	46.3	47.3	46.1	48.5	44.9	45.3	44.5	28.6	26.8	31.6	31.5	29.4	34.8	26.6	25.0	29.4
Same sex couples should have the right to legal marital status [1997]	47.5	49.9	44.7	39.9	43.1	36.7	52.5	54.1	50.5	46.7	49.5	42.0	39.8	43.0	34.5	51.3	53.8	47.1
The activities of married women are best confined to the home and family	46.0	41.3	50.7	55.4	49.0	62.0	38.2	35.0	41.4	27.6	25.4	31.5	33.8	31.9	37.1	23.5	21.1	27.6
The death penalty should be abolished	68.3	67.5	69.2	68.1	67.0	69.2	68.5	67.9	69.2	42.2	41.7	43.2	40.8	39.9	42.2	43.2	42.8	43.9
There is too much concern in the courts for the rights of criminals	31.9	30.1	33.8	35.4	33.8	37.0	29.0	26.9	31.1	48.7	48.9	48.4	51.3	51.6	50.8	46.9	47.0	46.8
How would you characterize your political views?																		
Far left	7.0	6.9	7.0	7.8	8.2	7.3	6.3	5.9	6.7	5.1	5.3	4.9	5.5	5.5	5.5	4.8	5.1	4.5
Liberal	42.7	45.9	39.5	43.8	47.9	39.6	41.8	44.2	39.4	30.6	31.1	29.8	27.1	28.1	25.3	33.0	33.1	32.9
Middle of the road	38.1	36.5	39.8	36.1	33.8	38.5	39.8	38.8	40.8	47.3	48.7	44.8	49.0	50.1	47.3	46.0	47.8	43.0
Conservative	10.8	9.6	12.1	10.9	9.3	12.5	10.7	9.7	11.7	14.9	13.3	17.6	16.1	14.4	18.9	14.1	12.6	16.6
Far right	1.4	1.1	1.7	1.4	0.8	2.1	1.4	1.3	1.4	2.1	1.6	3.0	2.3	2.0	3.0	2.0	1.4	3.0

Your probable career/occupation

ITEM	1971 ALL – ALL	1971 ALL – PWI	1971 ALL – HBCU	1971 MEN – ALL	1971 MEN – PWI	1971 MEN – HBCU	1971 WOMEN – ALL	1971 WOMEN – PWI	1971 WOMEN – HBCU	2004 ALL – ALL	2004 ALL – PWI	2004 ALL – HBCU	2004 MEN – ALL	2004 MEN – PWI	2004 MEN – HBCU	2004 WOMEN – ALL	2004 WOMEN – PWI	2004 WOMEN – HBCU
Accountant or actuary	4.1	3.7	4.4	5.2	4.8	5.8	3.2	2.9	3.5	3.0	2.8	3.4	2.9	2.8	3.0	3.1	2.8	3.6
Actor or entertainer	1.0	1.0	1.0	0.8	0.6	0.9	1.2	1.3	1.1	2.1	2.2	2.1	2.4	2.1	2.9	2.0	2.2	1.5
Architect	1.0	0.6	1.4	2.1	1.2	3.0	0.1	0.2	0.1	1.0	0.9	1.2	1.8	1.4	2.4	0.5	0.5	0.4
Artist	1.7	1.6	1.8	1.8	1.5	2.2	1.5	1.7	1.4	1.3	1.7	0.6	1.9	2.3	1.2	0.9	1.3	0.2
Business (clerical)	2.8	2.5	3.1	0.7	0.6	0.9	4.4	4.0	4.7	0.6	0.6	0.6	0.7	0.7	0.6	0.5	0.5	0.6
Business executive (management, administrator)	8.6	8.0	9.2	12.8	12.0	13.8	5.2	4.7	5.7	7.6	7.8	7.2	10.2	10.6	9.5	5.9	5.9	5.8
Business owner or proprietor	0.9	0.7	1.0	1.6	1.3	1.9	0.3	0.2	0.3	4.1	4.1	4.2	6.6	6.7	6.5	2.6	2.5	2.7
Business salesperson or buyer	0.4	0.3	0.5	0.5	0.3	0.7	0.3	0.3	0.3	0.7	0.7	0.7	0.9	0.9	0.9	0.6	0.6	0.7
Clergy (minister, priest)	0.2	0.3	0.1	0.5	0.6	0.3	0.0	0.0	0.0	0.1	0.1	0.1	0.2	0.3	0.1	0.0	0.1	0.0
Clergy (other religious)	0.1	0.1	0.0	0.1	0.1	0.1	0.1	0.1	0.0	0.0	0.1	0.0	0.0	0.1	0.0	0.1	0.1	0.0
Clinical psychologist	2.7	2.6	2.8	1.6	1.6	1.6	3.5	3.4	3.6	2.3	2.0	2.9	1.0	0.7	1.3	3.2	2.9	3.9
College administrator/staff	—	—	—	—	—	—	—	—	—	0.1	0.0	0.1	0.1	0.1	0.2	0.0	0.0	0.0
College teacher	1.8	1.6	2.0	1.6	1.6	1.6	2.0	1.7	2.3	0.3	0.3	0.2	0.4	0.4	0.4	0.3	0.3	0.2
Computer programmer or analyst	1.7	1.9	1.6	2.0	2.2	1.8	1.5	1.6	1.4	3.5	3.0	4.2	6.6	6.0	7.6	1.4	1.1	1.9
Conservationist or forester	0.1	0.1	0.1	0.2	0.2	0.1	0.0	0.0	0.0	0.1	0.1	0.1	0.1	0.1	0.0	0.1	0.0	0.1
Dentist (including orthodontist)	0.6	0.7	0.5	1.1	1.4	0.8	0.2	0.1	0.2	1.2	1.2	1.2	0.8	0.8	0.8	1.5	1.5	1.5
Dietitian or home economist	0.5	0.3	0.7	0.1	0.1	0.0	0.9	0.5	1.3	0.3	0.2	0.3	0.2	0.2	0.3	0.3	0.2	0.4
Engineer	4.2	5.3	3.0	8.8	10.9	6.4	0.5	0.7	0.4	6.1	5.7	6.8	11.8	10.9	13.4	2.4	2.3	2.6
Farmer or rancher	0.1	0.2	0.2	0.2	0.3	0.3	0.1	0.1	0.1	0.1	0.1	0.1	0.3	0.3	0.2	0.0	0.0	0.1
Foreign service worker (incl diplomat)	0.5	0.6	0.4	0.6	0.8	0.3	0.5	0.5	0.5	0.3	0.4	0.1	0.1	0.2	0.0	0.5	0.6	0.2
Homemaker (full-time)	0.2	0.1	0.3	0.1	0.1	0.2	0.3	0.2	0.4	0.0	0.0	0.0	0.0	0.0	0.0	0.1	0.1	0.0
Interior decorator (including designer)	0.8	0.7	0.8	0.3	0.2	0.3	1.1	1.1	1.2	0.3	0.4	0.1	0.0	0.0	0.1	0.4	0.6	0.2
Interpreter (translator)	0.3	0.4	0.2	0.1	0.1	0.3	0.4	0.6	0.3	—	—	—	—	—	—	—	—	—
Lab technician or hygienist	1.3	1.5	1.1	0.6	0.5	0.6	1.9	2.3	1.5	0.2	0.2	0.3	0.2	0.2	0.2	0.3	0.2	0.4
Law enforcement officer	0.4	0.5	0.2	0.7	0.9	0.4	0.1	0.2	0.1	0.9	0.9	0.9	1.6	1.7	1.6	0.5	0.5	0.5
Lawyer (attorney) or judge	7.0	8.1	5.8	10.8	12.2	9.2	4.0	4.7	3.2	6.1	6.0	6.2	4.3	4.5	3.8	7.2	6.9	7.8
Military service (career)	0.8	1.1	0.4	1.7	2.4	1.0	0.0	0.0	0.0	0.5	0.5	0.6	0.9	0.9	1.0	0.2	0.2	0.3
Musician (performer, composer)	2.0	1.3	2.8	2.9	1.9	4.0	1.3	0.7	1.9	1.6	1.5	1.7	2.5	2.4	2.8	0.9	0.9	1.0
Nurse	4.2	5.2	3.1	0.1	0.1	0.0	7.4	9.3	5.4	6.2	5.8	7.1	0.9	1.0	0.8	9.7	8.8	11.2
Optometrist	0.0	0.0	0.0	0.0	0.0	0.0	0.0	0.0	0.0	0.3	0.4	0.1	0.2	0.2	0.1	0.4	0.5	0.1
Pharmacist	0.7	1.1	0.3	0.7	1.1	0.3	0.7	1.1	0.2	3.1	2.6	4.0	2.7	2.0	4.1	3.3	2.9	3.9
Physician	4.9	5.9	3.7	6.4	7.7	4.9	3.6	4.5	2.8	10.0	9.8	10.3	6.5	5.9	7.4	12.3	12.3	12.3
Policymaker/government	—	—	—	—	—	—	—	—	—	0.7	0.9	0.5	0.9	1.1	0.6	0.6	0.7	0.4
School counselor	0.9	0.7	1.1	0.4	0.4	0.5	1.2	0.9	1.6	0.3	0.3	0.3	0.2	0.2	0.3	0.4	0.4	0.3
School principal or superintendent	0.2	0.2	0.1	0.3	0.3	0.2	0.1	0.1	0.1	0.1	0.1	0.1	0.0	0.1	0.0	0.2	0.1	0.2
Scientific researcher	1.9	2.3	1.4	2.5	3.0	1.9	1.4	1.7	1.0	1.1	1.3	0.9	1.2	1.2	1.3	1.0	1.3	0.6
Social, welfare or recreation worker	7.5	6.0	9.2	4.6	3.6	5.6	9.9	7.9	11.8	1.4	1.1	2.0	0.6	0.3	1.0	2.0	1.6	2.7
Statistician	0.1	0.2	0.1	0.2	0.3	0.1	0.1	0.0	0.2	—	—	—	—	—	—	—	—	—
Therapist (physical, occupational, speech)	2.1	1.8	2.4	0.6	0.7	0.6	3.2	2.7	3.7	3.0	2.8	3.3	2.4	2.2	2.9	3.3	3.2	3.6
Teacher or administrator (elementary)	7.5	6.2	8.9	1.7	1.0	2.4	12.1	10.5	13.7	3.4	3.2	3.9	1.2	1.3	1.2	4.9	4.5	5.6
Teacher or administrator (secondary)	8.5	7.1	10.0	7.7	5.6	10.1	9.1	8.3	9.9	2.4	2.8	1.7	2.7	3.0	2.2	2.2	2.6	1.4
Veterinarian	0.3	0.5	0.2	0.6	0.9	0.3	0.1	0.1	0.1	1.0	0.8	1.2	0.5	0.5	0.6	1.3	1.1	1.6
Writer or journalist	1.6	1.9	1.3	0.9	0.9	0.9	2.2	2.8	1.5	2.3	2.7	1.6	1.6	1.9	1.1	2.8	3.2	2.0
Skilled trades	0.5	0.7	0.3	0.7	0.9	0.6	0.3	0.5	0.1	0.1	0.1	0.1	0.2	0.2	0.1	0.1	0.1	0.1
Other	5.3	5.6	4.9	4.9	5.2	4.4	5.6	5.9	5.3	11.4	11.8	10.6	9.4	10.2	8.1	12.6	12.9	12.2
Undecided	8.4	8.8	7.9	8.3	7.8	8.8	8.5	9.7	7.2	8.7	10.1	6.3	10.1	11.6	7.5	7.8	9.1	5.5

ITEM	1971 ALL·ALL	1971 ALL·PWI	1971 ALL·HBCU	1971 MEN·ALL	1971 MEN·PWI	1971 MEN·HBCU	1971 WOMEN·ALL	1971 WOMEN·PWI	1971 WOMEN·HBCU	2004 ALL·ALL	2004 ALL·PWI	2004 ALL·HBCU	2004 MEN·ALL	2004 MEN·PWI	2004 MEN·HBCU	2004 WOMEN·ALL	2004 WOMEN·PWI	2004 WOMEN·HBCU
Student's probable major																		
Arts and Humanities																		
Art, fine and applied	2.2	2.4	1.9	2.0	1.8	2.4	2.3	2.9	1.5	1.8	2.2	1.1	2.1	2.4	1.6	1.5	2.0	0.7
English (language and literature)	2.4	2.4	2.4	0.7	0.7	0.7	3.8	3.7	3.8	1.2	1.3	1.0	0.6	0.6	0.6	1.5	1.7	1.3
History	3.3	2.5	4.2	4.1	3.2	5.1	2.6	1.9	3.4	0.5	0.7	0.3	0.5	0.8	0.1	0.5	0.6	0.3
Journalism	1.3	1.6	0.9	0.7	0.8	0.5	1.7	2.2	1.3	1.8	2.2	1.0	1.2	1.5	0.6	2.2	2.7	1.3
Language and Literature (except English)	0.9	1.2	0.6	0.6	0.9	0.3	1.1	1.4	0.8	0.3	0.4	0.1	0.1	0.2	0.0	0.3	0.5	0.1
Music	3.1	2.5	3.7	3.6	2.6	4.6	2.7	2.5	2.9	1.4	1.3	1.5	2.1	2.0	2.3	0.9	0.9	0.9
Philosophy	0.4	0.5	0.4	0.6	0.6	0.5	0.3	0.3	0.3	0.2	0.2	0.0	0.2	0.3	0.1	0.2	0.2	0.0
Speech or Theater	1.2	1.3	1.0	0.5	0.6	0.4	1.7	2.0	1.5	—	—	—	—	—	—	—	—	—
Theater or Drama	—	—	—	—	—	—	—	—	—	1.0	1.3	0.6	0.8	1.0	0.5	1.2	1.5	0.6
Speech	—	—	—	—	—	—	—	—	—	0.1	0.1	0.2	0.1	0.1	0.2	0.2	0.2	0.1
Theology or Religion	0.3	0.5	0.1	0.6	0.9	0.3	0.0	0.1	0.0	0.1	0.1	0.0	0.2	0.3	0.0	0.1	0.1	0.1
Other Arts and Humanities	0.5	0.6	0.5	0.3	0.2	0.3	0.7	0.9	0.5	0.8	1.0	0.4	0.5	0.7	0.1	0.9	1.1	0.6
Biological Science																		
Biology (general)	2.2	2.0	2.4	2.7	2.6	2.7	1.8	1.5	2.1	7.0	6.1	8.6	5.1	3.9	7.1	8.3	7.6	9.5
Biochemistry or Biophysics	0.5	0.5	0.4	0.7	0.8	0.6	0.3	0.4	0.2	0.8	1.0	0.5	0.6	0.7	0.5	0.9	1.1	0.6
Botany	0.0	0.0	0.1	0.1	0.0	0.1	0.0	0.1	0.0	0.0	0.0	0.0	0.0	0.0	0.0	0.0	0.0	0.0
Environmental Science	0.0	0.1	0.0	0.1	0.1	0.0	0.0	0.0	0.0	0.1	0.1	0.1	0.1	0.1	0.2	0.1	0.1	0.0
Marine (life) Science	—	—	—	—	—	—	—	—	—	0.2	0.2	0.3	0.4	0.2	0.7	0.1	0.2	0.1
Microbiology or Bacteriology	—	—	—	—	—	—	—	—	—	0.2	0.3	0.1	0.3	0.3	0.0	0.3	0.4	0.1
Zoology	0.2	0.2	0.2	0.3	0.2	0.4	0.2	0.2	0.1	0.2	0.1	0.3	0.3	0.3	0.4	0.1	0.1	0.2
Other Biological Science	0.3	0.3	0.3	0.4	0.3	0.6	0.2	0.3	0.1	0.7	0.8	0.6	0.7	0.7	0.7	0.7	0.8	0.6
Business																		
Accounting	3.7	3.3	4.2	5.0	4.3	5.6	2.7	2.4	3.1	2.9	2.8	3.2	3.1	3.1	3.0	2.8	2.6	3.2
Business Administration (general)	10.4	9.4	11.6	15.0	13.8	16.3	6.8	5.7	8.0	4.4	3.9	5.1	6.1	5.5	7.2	3.2	2.9	3.7
Finance	—	—	—	—	—	—	—	—	—	1.4	1.6	1.1	2.1	2.4	1.6	1.0	1.1	0.8
International Business	—	—	—	—	—	—	—	—	—	1.0	1.3	0.5	1.1	1.5	0.5	1.0	1.2	0.5
Marketing	—	—	—	—	—	—	—	—	—	3.1	3.2	2.9	3.7	3.7	3.8	2.6	2.8	2.3
Management	—	—	—	—	—	—	—	—	—	4.6	4.6	4.6	7.1	7.4	6.7	3.0	2.8	3.2
Secretarial Studies	2.3	2.4	2.1	0.0	0.0	0.0	4.0	4.4	3.7	0.0	0.0	0.0	0.0	0.0	0.0	0.0	0.0	0.0
Other Business	0.8	0.7	0.8	0.7	0.9	0.6	0.8	0.6	1.1	0.8	0.9	0.5	1.0	1.3	0.5	0.7	0.7	0.5
Education																		
Business Education	—	—	—	—	—	—	—	—	—	0.3	0.2	0.4	0.3	0.3	0.3	0.3	0.2	0.5
Elementary Education	—	—	—	—	—	—	—	—	—	3.5	3.2	4.0	1.3	1.4	1.1	4.9	4.4	5.9
Music or Art Education	—	—	—	—	—	—	—	—	—	0.3	0.3	0.4	0.4	0.5	0.4	0.2	0.4	0.4
Physical Education or Recreation	3.8	2.7	5.0	5.3	3.2	7.6	2.7	2.4	3.0	1.0	1.0	0.9	2.1	2.1	2.0	0.3	0.3	0.2
Secondary Education	—	—	—	—	—	—	—	—	—	1.5	1.7	1.2	1.5	1.6	1.3	1.6	1.8	1.2
Special Education	—	—	—	—	—	—	—	—	—	0.3	0.2	0.3	0.2	0.1	0.2	0.3	0.3	0.4
Other Education	7.5	6.4	8.6	1.8	1.4	2.3	11.9	10.4	13.5	0.4	0.3	0.5	0.2	0.3	0.2	0.5	0.3	0.7
Engineering																		
Aeronautical or Astronautical Eng	0.4	0.6	0.2	0.9	1.3	0.4	0.0	0.0	0.0	0.7	0.5	0.9	1.3	1.1	1.7	0.2	0.2	0.3
Civil Engineering	0.5	0.5	0.4	1.0	1.1	0.9	0.1	0.1	0.1	0.6	0.7	0.5	1.1	1.2	1.0	0.3	0.3	0.1
Chemical Engineering	0.3	0.4	0.2	0.6	0.9	0.3	0.0	0.0	0.1	0.6	0.5	0.8	0.8	0.7	1.0	0.5	0.4	0.6
Electrical or Electronic Engineering	1.5	1.7	1.3	3.2	3.6	2.8	0.1	0.1	0.1	1.6	1.1	2.3	3.4	2.4	5.1	0.3	0.2	0.5
Industrial Engineering	0.4	0.6	0.3	1.0	1.2	0.8	0.0	0.0	0.0	0.2	0.2	0.2	0.3	0.3	0.3	0.1	0.1	0.1
Mechanical Engineering	1.1	1.6	0.5	2.2	3.1	1.2	0.2	0.3	0.0	1.6	1.5	1.7	3.5	3.2	3.9	0.4	0.4	0.3
Other Engineering	0.3	0.4	0.3	0.5	0.7	0.3	0.1	0.1	0.2	2.5	2.9	1.8	4.7	5.6	3.2	1.1	1.2	0.9

Student's probable undergraduate field

ITEM	1971 ALL			1971 MEN			1971 WOMEN			2004 ALL			2004 MEN			2004 WOMEN		
	ALL	PWI	HBCU	ALL	PWI	HBCU	ALL	PWI	HBCU	ALL	PWI	HBCU	ALL	PWI	HBCU	ALL	PWI	HBCU
Physical Science																		
Astronomy	—	—	—	—	—	—	—	—	—	0.1	0.1	0.1	0.1	0.1	0.2	0.1	0.0	0.1
Atmospheric Science (incl Meteorology)	—	—	—	—	—	—	—	—	—	0.0	0.0	0.0	0.0	0.1	0.0	0.0	0.0	0.0
Chemistry	0.9	1.0	0.8	1.1	1.3	0.9	0.8	0.8	0.8	1.2	1.1	1.3	1.0	1.0	1.0	1.3	1.2	1.5
Earth Science	0.1	0.0	0.2	0.1	0.1	0.2	0.1	0.0	0.2	0.1	0.0	0.0	0.0	0.1	0.1	0.0	0.0	0.0
Marine Science	—	—	—	—	—	—	—	—	—	0.1	0.0	0.1	0.1	0.0	0.1	0.1	0.0	0.1
Mathematics	2.7	3.0	2.3	2.4	2.7	2.1	2.9	3.3	2.4	0.4	0.4	0.4	0.6	0.5	0.6	0.4	0.4	0.3
Physics	0.4	0.4	0.3	0.6	0.8	0.5	0.2	0.1	0.2	0.3	0.3	0.2	0.5	0.6	0.4	0.1	0.2	0.1
Statistics	0.0	0.0	0.0	0.0	0.1	0.0	0.0	0.0	0.0	0.0	0.0	0.0	0.0	0.0	0.0	0.0	0.0	0.0
Other Physical Science	0.0	0.0	0.0	0.0	0.0	0.0	0.0	0.0	0.1	0.1	0.1	0.2	0.1	0.1	0.1	0.1	0.1	0.2
Professional																		
Architecture or Urban Planning	1.0	0.8	1.2	2.2	1.7	2.7	0.1	0.2	0.1	0.7	0.6	0.7	1.1	1.1	1.2	0.4	0.4	0.4
Home Economics	1.5	1.0	2.0	0.0	0.1	0.0	2.7	1.8	3.5	0.1	0.1	0.1	0.0	0.0	0.1	0.1	0.1	0.0
Health Technology (medical, dental, laboratory)	1.6	2.1	1.0	1.1	1.5	0.7	1.9	2.6	1.2	0.6	0.8	0.4	0.4	0.4	0.4	0.8	1.0	0.5
Library or Archival Science	0.2	0.2	0.2	0.0	0.0	0.0	0.3	0.4	0.3	0.0	0.0	0.0	0.0	0.0	0.0	0.0	0.0	0.0
Medical, Dental, Veterinary	4.6	5.9	3.3	6.1	7.9	4.2	3.5	4.4	2.6	6.0	6.4	5.5	3.3	3.4	3.2	7.8	8.3	6.9
Nursing	4.2	5.4	3.0	0.1	0.2	0.1	7.4	9.6	5.2	6.4	6.1	7.1	0.8	0.9	0.7	10.1	9.4	11.4
Pharmacy	0.5	0.8	0.2	0.5	0.6	0.3	0.6	0.9	0.1	2.3	1.8	3.2	2.0	1.4	3.0	2.6	2.1	3.3
Therapy (occupational, physical, speech)	2.1	2.0	2.1	0.7	0.6	0.8	3.2	3.1	3.2	2.4	2.2	2.7	2.1	1.9	2.4	2.6	2.4	2.9
Other Professional	0.5	0.5	0.5	0.3	0.3	0.3	0.7	0.6	0.7	0.9	1.0	0.6	0.8	0.8	0.7	0.9	1.1	0.6
Social Science																		
Anthropology	0.2	0.3	0.1	0.2	0.2	0.1	0.2	0.3	0.0	0.1	0.2	0.0	0.0	0.1	0.0	0.2	0.3	0.0
Economics	0.6	0.5	0.7	0.8	0.6	0.9	0.5	0.4	0.5	0.4	0.4	0.5	0.4	0.5	0.1	0.5	0.3	0.7
Ethnic Studies	—	—	—	—	—	—	—	—	—	0.1	0.1	0.0	0.1	0.2	0.1	0.0	0.1	0.0
Geography	0.0	0.0	0.0	0.0	0.0	0.0	0.0	0.0	0.0	0.0	0.0	0.0	0.0	0.0	0.0	0.0	0.0	0.0
Political science (gov't, international relations)	3.0	2.5	3.4	4.4	3.8	5.0	1.9	1.5	2.2	3.2	3.1	3.2	2.8	2.9	2.5	3.4	3.2	3.7
Psychology	5.9	5.8	5.9	4.0	4.5	3.5	7.3	6.9	7.8	6.7	6.6	6.9	3.2	3.3	3.2	9.0	8.7	9.5
Social Work	4.1	3.7	4.5	1.9	1.6	2.3	5.8	5.4	6.2	1.1	0.8	1.7	0.5	0.2	0.9	1.6	1.1	2.3
Sociology	4.5	3.3	5.8	4.1	3.0	5.2	4.9	3.6	6.2	0.9	0.8	1.1	0.6	0.5	0.8	1.1	0.9	1.4
Women's Studies	—	—	—	—	—	—	—	—	—	0.0	0.0	0.0	0.0	0.0	0.0	0.0	0.1	0.0
Other Social Science	0.1	0.1	0.1	0.1	0.1	0.1	0.1	0.1	0.1	0.3	0.3	0.3	0.2	0.3	0.1	0.4	0.3	0.4
Technical																		
Building Trades	0.3	0.2	0.5	0.6	0.2	1.2	0.1	0.2	0.0	0.0	0.0	0.0	0.0	0.0	0.0	0.0	0.0	0.0
Data Processing or Computer Programming	0.9	0.9	0.9	1.1	1.5	1.2	0.5	0.5	0.6	0.9	0.8	1.0	1.7	1.6	1.9	0.3	0.2	0.5
Drafting or Design	—	—	—	—	—	—	—	—	—	0.4	0.5	0.3	0.7	0.8	0.6	0.3	0.3	0.2
Electronics	0.3	0.2	0.3	0.6	0.5	0.7	0.0	0.1	0.0	0.2	0.2	0.2	0.3	0.3	0.4	0.1	0.1	0.0
Mechanics	—	—	—	—	—	—	—	—	—	0.0	0.0	0.1	0.1	0.0	0.2	0.0	0.0	0.0
Other Technical	0.3	0.3	0.2	0.3	0.3	0.2	0.0	0.2	0.2	0.1	0.1	0.1	0.2	0.3	0.2	0.0	0.0	0.0
Other																		
Agriculture	0.3	0.1	0.6	0.6	0.2	1.2	0.1	0.1	0.2	0.2	0.1	0.3	0.2	0.1	0.4	0.2	0.1	0.3
Communications (radio, TV, etc.)	0.7	0.7	0.7	1.1	1.1	1.0	0.4	0.4	0.4	2.2	2.2	2.2	2.4	2.1	2.8	2.1	2.3	1.7
Computer Science	0.8	1.0	0.5	0.8	1.1	0.6	0.7	1.0	0.4	2.5	1.9	3.4	4.4	3.5	5.9	1.2	0.9	1.7
Forestry	0.0	0.0	0.0	0.0	0.0	0.1	0.0	0.0	0.0	0.0	0.0	0.1	0.0	0.0	0.1	0.0	0.0	0.1
Law Enforcement	—	—	—	—	—	—	—	—	—	1.3	1.3	1.2	1.6	1.8	1.2	1.1	1.0	1.3
Military Science	0.2	0.3	0.0	0.5	0.8	0.1	0.0	0.0	0.0	0.0	0.0	0.0	0.0	0.0	0.1	0.0	0.0	0.0
Other field	4.9	6.7	3.1	7.3	10.1	4.4	3.0	3.9	2.1	2.1	2.5	1.5	1.9	2.3	1.2	2.3	2.6	1.7
Undecided	1.0	1.0	0.9	0.9	1.0	0.7	1.1	1.1	1.1	3.9	4.7	2.6	4.1	5.1	2.6	3.7	4.4	2.7

Higher Education Research Institute
Publications List

Race and Ethnicity in the American Professoriate, 1995–96

Highlights findings and draws comparisons between various racial and ethnic groups of faculty. Faculty's views and values about undergraduate education, professional goals and institutional climate are examined along with preferred teaching and evaluation methods, levels of work satisfaction and sources of stress.

April, 1997/141 pages $25.00   □

The American College Teacher

Provides an informative profile of teaching faculty at American colleges and universities. Teaching, research activities and professional development issues are highlighted along with issues related to job satisfaction and stress.

National Norms for 2004–05 HERI Faculty Survey report.
    September, 2005/156 pages $25.00   □
National Norms for 2001–02 HERI Faculty Survey report.
    September, 2002/146 pages $25.00   □
National Norms for 1998–99 HERI Faculty Survey report.
    September, 1999/128 pages $22.00   □
National Norms for 1995–96 HERI Faculty Survey report.
    September, 1996/127 pages $22.00   □
National Norms for 1992–93 HERI Faculty Survey report.
    September, 1993/107 pages $20.00   □

Degree Attainment Rates at American Colleges and Universities

Provides latest information on four- and six-year degree attainment rates collected longitudinally from 262 baccalaureate-granting institutions. Differences by race, gender, and institutional type are examined. The study highlights main predictors of degree completion and provides several formulas for calculating expected institutional completion rates. The study also provides a section on trends in degree attainment in the last decade.

November, 2002/77 pages $15.00   □

Black Undergraduates From *Bakke* to *Grutter*

Summarizes the status, trends and prospects of Black college freshmen using data collected from 1971 to 2004 through the Cooperative Institutional Research Program (CIRP). Based on more than half a million Black freshman students, the report examines gender differences; socioeconomic status; academic preparation and aspirations; and civic engagement.

November, 2005/47 pages $15.00   □

The American Freshman: Thirty-Five Year Trends

Summarizes trends in the CIRP survey data between 1966 and 2001, stressing trends in the past half-decade. The report examines changes in family structure; parental income and students' financial concerns, as well as gender differences in educational plans and career aspirations, behaviors and values. Academic trends include: increases in grade inflation and graduate degree aspirations. Trends in students' political and social attitudes are also covered.

December, 2002/222 pages $30.00   □

The American Freshman

Provides national normative data on the characteristics of students attending American colleges and universities as first-time, full-time freshmen. In 2004, data from approximately 300,000 freshmen students are statistically adjusted to reflect the responses of 1.3 million students entering college. The annual report covers: demographic characteristics; expectations of college; degree goals and career plans; college finances; attitudes, values and life goals.

    December, 2004/188 pages $25.00   □
    December, 2003/186 pages $25.00   □
    December, 2002/189 pages $25.00   □
    December, 2001   (out of stock)
    December, 2000/187 pages $25.00   □
    December, 1999/181 pages $25.00   □
    December, 1998   (out of stock)
    December, 1997/181 pages $22.00   □

Note: National norms for most years between 1966–1996 are available.

The American College Student

Provides information on the college student experience two and four years after college entry. Student satisfaction, talent development, student involvement, changing values and career development, and retention issues are highlighted along with normative data from student responses to the HERI Follow-up Surveys.

1990 report: Normative Data for 1986 and 1988 College Freshmen
October, 1991/196 pages $15.00   □

1988 report: Normative Data for 1984 and 1986 College Freshmen
August, 1990/210 pages $15.00   □

To Order: send this form with a check to:
The Higher Education Research Institute
UCLA Graduate School of Education and Information Studies
Mailbox 951521
Los Angeles, CA 90095-1521
(Add $5.00 for shipping, plus $1.00 for each additional book ordered)

HERI accepts Visa, MasterCard & Discover: Call (310) 825-1925 to order by credit card
Or visit the HERI webpage: www.gseis.ucla.edu/heri/heri.html